Dodgers

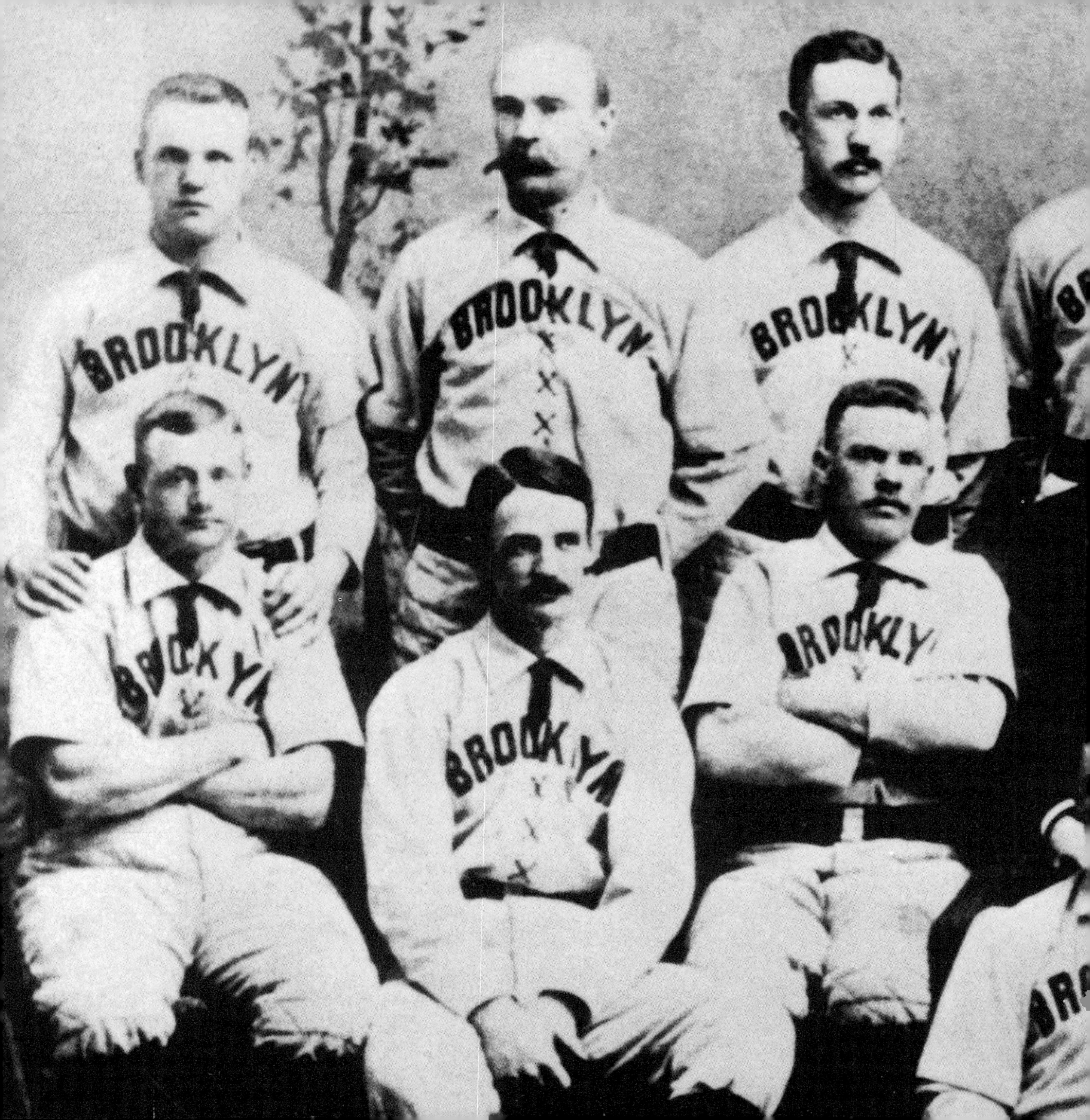
BROOKLYN
BROOKLYN
BROOKLYN

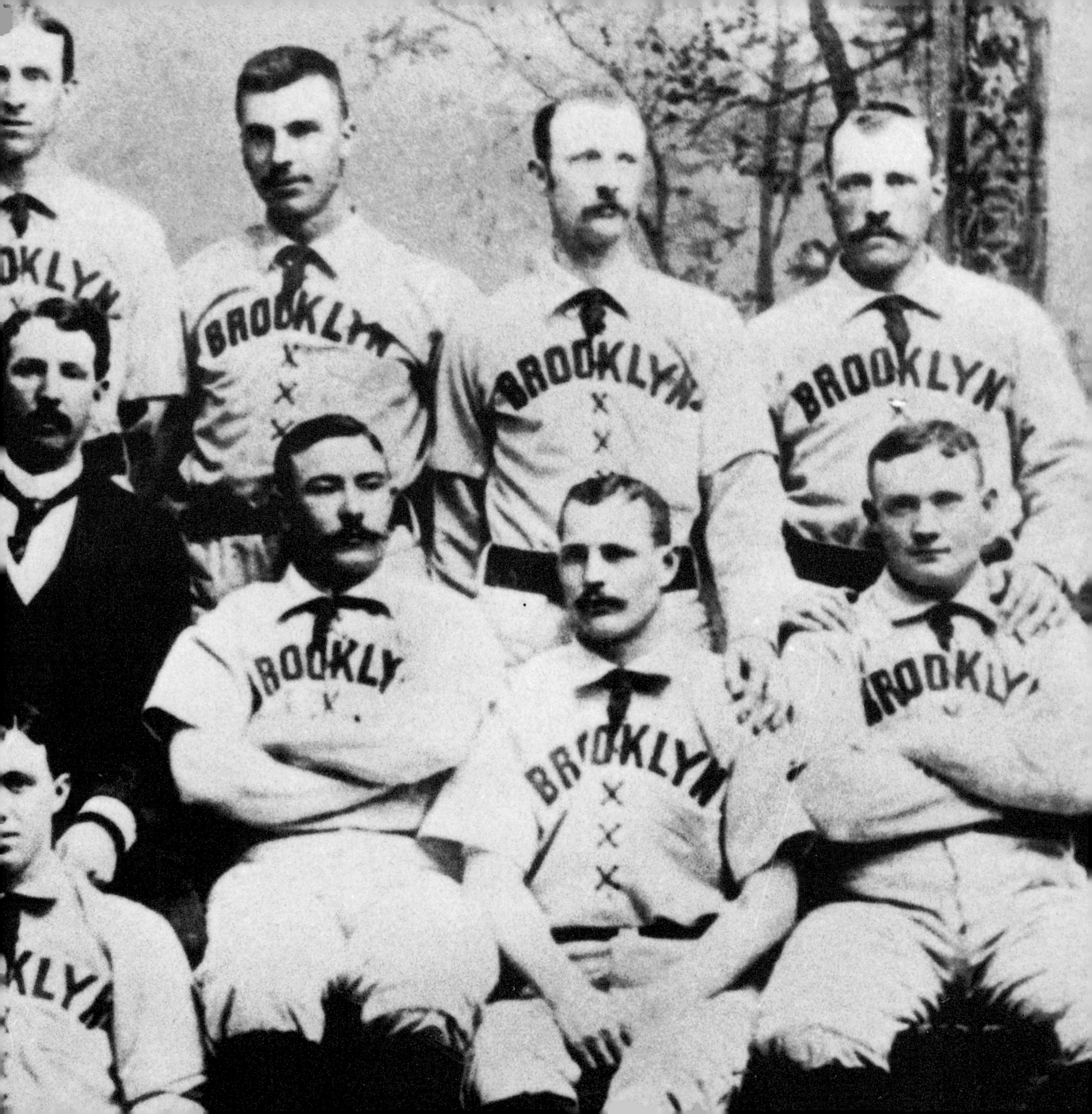
BROOKLYN
BROOKLYN
BROOKLYN

THE DODGERS

**MEMORIES AND
MEMORABILIA FROM
BROOKLYN TO L.A.**

Text by Bruce Chadwick
Photography by David M. Spindel

ABBEVILLE PRESS • PUBLISHERS
New York • London • Paris

Front cover, clockwise from upper right: 1963 World Series program (p. 104), ball signed by Durocher, Robinson, Reese, and others (p. 81), Dodgers at a triumphant 1947 spring training (p. 70), Robinson card (p. 147), doll and ball commemorating 1940 team (p. 56), Nap Rucker "blanket" (p. 27).

Back cover, clockwise from upper right: Ebbets Field postcard with Dodger button (p. 40), Koufax after fourth no-hitter (p. 108), pin from L.A.'s first World Series (p. 99), Lasorda in celebration (p. 125), Robinson and Reese hitting instruction record (p. 67), L.A. patch (p. 138), 1963 Dodger banner (p. 107).

Pages 2–3: The Dodgers, 1890 (p. 19). Frontispiece: Dodger memories, Brooklyn style. Title page: left, World Series pin (p. 139) and 1884 scorecard (p. 18). Pages 8–9, counterclockwise from upper left: 1962 Dodger Stadium grand opening pennant (p. 118), two Dodger pins (p. 30), Jackie Robinson doll (p. 84), Ebbets Field opening day 1941 ticket (p. 53), signed 1957 Dodger poster (p. 96), 1965 World Series program and tickets (p. 111), signed team bat (p. 139), 1959 World Series ticket (p. 88).

To Margie and Rory.

—B.C.

EDITOR: Constance Herndon
DESIGNERS: Patricia Fabricant and Virginia Pope
PRODUCTION EDITOR: Robin James
PRODUCTION SUPERVISOR: Simone René

To my mother, Hilda, who created me, and to my mother-in-law, Rose, who created my wife and sparked my interest in collecting memorabilia.

—D.M.S.

Library of Congress Cataloging-in-Publication Data
Chadwick, Bruce.
    The Dodgers: memories and memorabilia from Brooklyn to L.A./
    text by Bruce Chadwick : photography by David M. Spindel.
        p.   cm.
    Includes bibliographical references (p.   ) and index
    ISBN 1-55859-380-2
    1. Brooklyn Dodgers (Baseball team)—History.   2. Los Angeles Dodgers (Baseball team)—History.   I. Title.
GV875.B7C43   1993
796.357'64'0974723—dc20   92-37341
                                                       CIP

ACKNOWLEDGMENTS

I t seems as if every other person in the United States is a Dodger fan, but finding great Dodger memorabilia has not been easy. Many people have some memorabilia, but few have the priceless pieces a book like this requires. Finding the souvenirs was a wonderful treasure hunt for us, and we want to thank the different collectors who let us photograph their collections. We are particularly grateful to Rafael Sanchez in Los Angeles and Sal LaRocca in New York. Thanks also to Josh Evans, president of Lelands, Inc., the New York sports auction house, and to the hard-working researchers at the National Baseball Hall of Fame in Cooperstown, New York, particularly its photo director, Patricia Kelly. We would also like to express our appreciation to Brent Shyer and the staff of the Los Angeles Dodgers.

In addition, we'd also like to thank the athletes and sports personalities who talked to us, particularly Ralph Branca, Duke Snider, Cal Abrams, Daryll Strawberry, Tommy Lasorda, Don Drysdale, Don Newcombe, Maury Wills, and Gary Carter.

Finally, our special thanks go to Constance Herndon, our editor, as well as Patricia Fabricant and Virginia Pope, our designers, who helped us tell the story of the Dodgers.

—BRUCE CHADWICK AND DAVID M. SPINDEL

CONTENTS

1957 Brooklyn Dodger Reunion

DODGER BLUE

The Dodgers are not the Los Angeles Dodgers, the Brooklyn Dodgers, the West Coast Dodgers, or the East Coast Dodgers—they are, simply, the Dodgers. American sports has never seen anything like them. They were, and are, originals, like Bobby Jones was in golf and Muhammad Ali in boxing. The Dodgers have always had a certain something you could never put your finger on, a charm and bravado, an unbelievable crowd appeal that no one else ever had.

The Tigers were named after the tough guys of the jungle, the Royals after kings, the Orioles, Cardinals, and Blue Jays after beautiful birds, the Rangers after folk heroes, the Twins after prosperous cities, the Angels after heavenly hosts, the Mariners after seafaring heroes, and the Astros after space explorers. The Dodgers were named after fans who had to dodge the trolley cars that were killing one fan a week at the turn of the century in Brooklyn.

Other teams had great base runners like Rickey Henderson, Vince Coleman, Ty Cobb, and Lou Brock. The Dodgers had Babe Herman, who was passed by runners on the base paths two times in one week. Once the team wound up with three runners standing on the same base. The Yankees had the graceful Joe DiMaggio, who could spear fly balls no matter where they fell from the azure sky. The Dodgers had third baseman

The most beloved stadium ever built followed by the most beautiful— from Brooklyn to Los Angeles, the Dodgers have played in style.

11

These tickets are reminders of the last glory years in Brooklyn, the late 1940s and 1950s, when Brooklyn ruled the National League

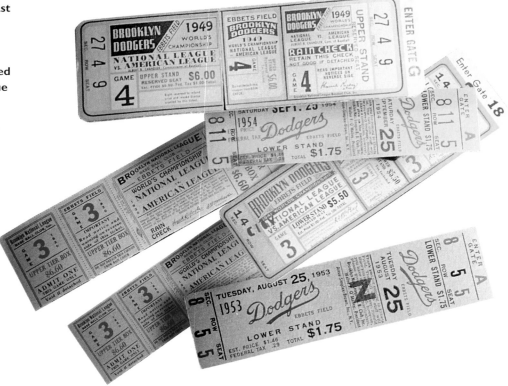

Billy Cox, who, when he let a grounder go through his legs, told the press, "I lost it in the sun."

The team has an enchanting history filled with marvelous characters who always seemed to be involved in extraordinary events. When they were good, as they have often been since the Forties, they were glorious. When they were bad, they were incredible. Only the Dodgers would sign a pitcher named Wild Bill Donovan, whose records for walks and wild pitches in a season stand to this day. Only the Dodgers could open their ballpark and forget to build a press box, forget the keys to the outfield gates, and have players and executives march out to center field to raise the American flag only to forget the flag. Only the Dodgers could be nicknamed "the Bums" when they were on the skids and be loved for it.

But the Dodgers also did things that

transformed baseball and enriched the nation forever. It was the Dodgers, along with the Giants, who brought major league baseball to the West Coast and, despite howls back in New York, truly made the game the coast-to-coast national pastime. And, most importantly, it was the Dodgers who broke the disgraceful color line and put Jackie Robinson into their regular lineup in 1947, opening the door to integration in baseball and, symbolically, in America.

Reeling from the transplant from bandbox Ebbets to the cavernous L.A. Coliseum, the Dodgers went from seventh place to first, and then, over the last 33 years, established a dynasty with nine pennants and five world championships. In Los Angeles, the Dodgers have regularly set attendance records. The O'Malleys have developed perhaps the country's best and most organized farm club system. In Los Angeles, the Dodgers, truly a West Coast team by 1962, gave fans a whole new pantheon of diamond heroes.

This book is the story of both the Brooklyn Dodgers and the Los Angeles Dodgers, of Oyster Burns, Pee Wee, the Duke, Wild Bill, Rube, Jackie, Campy, Newk, Sandy, Babe, Cookie, Brickyard, Nap, Zack, Ivy, Big D, Uncle Robbie, Casey, Dazzy, Dolph, Lefty, Ducky, Dixie, Leo the Lip, Preacher, and Van Lingle Mungo. And it is dedicated to all the fans who bleed Dodger blue, whether they got to the ballpark on the subway or the freeway.

1970 DODGER SCORECARD
25¢

A hulking Dodger signs for a kid on this 1970 scorecard.

A TEAM GROWS IN BROOKLYN
1884–1920

There is a well-worn myth that baseball was only played in the pastures of rural America before the turn of the century and that the game was so successful there that entrepreneurs later moved it into cities. That was never true. Baseball was played in the shadows of tall brick city buildings in Cincinnati at the same time it was played in front of barns in Pennsylvania. The game was as beloved in cities like New York and Boston as it was in towns along the Ohio River.

In fact, baseball in the middle of the nineteenth century was even more popular in busy, crowded cities than in small towns because cities had become havens for the millions of immigrants from Europe. The new arrivals, many of whom did not yet speak English, needed a game fans could follow and athletes could play without understanding a complex set of rules. Immigrants were also attracted to a game that would allow one ethnic group to challenge another and bring thousands of fans to the fray. Baseball was perfect.

Cities in the mid-nineteenth century were generally not as congested as they are now and playing fields were relatively easy to find, just as they were in small towns. But cities, unlike small towns, had populations large enough to make baseball a big attraction and later a business, plus ferries and trolley cars made transportation to and from playing fields

The 1890 Dodgers won the pennant in their very first season in the National League.

15

easy. Cities loved baseball, and no city in America loved the game more than Brooklyn.

A hundred years before the Dodgers fled Red Hook, Williamsburg, Flatbush, and other busy neighborhoods in the world's most written about borough, baseball thrived in Brooklyn. The first clubs were

A turn-of-the-century catcher's mask and 1890s souvenir bat anchor this collection of old Dodgers memorabilia.

formed in 1852 and by the beginning of the Civil War, Brooklyn had 71 different amateur teams. (Across the river, New York City had only 25.) Brooklyn's powerhouse team of the 1850s, the Eckfords, was made up of rough-and-tumble mechanics and shipwrights (as opposed to a fabled New York team, the Knickerbockers, which was made up of "gentlemen"). Soot covered, blue collar factory teams as well as neighborhood squads played each other all over Brooklyn, and the games attracted thousands of loud and howling fans.

Brooklyn became famous for its eccentric Dodgers in later years, but the area always was home to the unusual, the colorful, and the bizarre. The borough, then a separate city, was the site of the first baseball riot, in 1860, when a rhubarb broke out between players and fans of the Atlantics and Excelsiors. The first player to die from baseball (James Creighton) expired in Brooklyn in 1862 when he ruptured his bladder during a game. In 1861 Brooklynites played baseball on ice skates. In 1866 pitcher Candy Cummings threw the first curve ball in Brooklyn. The first base-stealing slide was made in Brooklyn in the 1870s.

Sensing baseball's popularity and sensing money, a local Brooklyn entrepreneur, William Cammeyer, built the

"Cabinet" cards such as these, so called because they were displayed in cabinets, were popular in the 1880s.

country's first enclosed ballpark, Union Grounds, in 1862 and was soon charging fifty cents a ticket to see Brooklyn's finest play. Shortly afterward, another entrepreneur built Capitoline Grounds, another enclosed stadium, in the Bedford-Stuyvesant area. It was home to baseball on ice in winter for a small league of teams, Phineas T. Barnum's circus in spring, and organized baseball in summer —an altogether proper mix. Permanent stadiums attracted dozens of teams, and baseball events soon became news, recorded in depth by local newspapers. Henry Chadwick, the "Father of Baseball" who invented scoring and the newspaper box score, reigned as sports editor of the *Brooklyn Eagle*. A sport was growing.

Baseball boomed after the Civil War and in 1876 the National League was formed. The league welcomed a New

York– anchored team, the Mutuals, who played their games at Brooklyn's Union Grounds. But the team was constantly in trouble for suspected game fixing. Finally, to save money, the Mutuals' owner canceled a road trip and was kicked out of the league. A Hartford, Connecticut, team took its place, moving to New York at Union Grounds, but it went bankrupt when fans refused to support it. A third New York team, the Metropolitans from Manhattan, were admitted later and eventually became the Giants.

Finally, frustrated at the lack of big-league ball in Brooklyn, in 1883 local real estate magnate and gambling hall operator Charles Byrne built Washington Park and imported a minor league team from Trenton, New Jersey.

From the start Byrne's team drew well, and in 1884 joined the American

17

fielder Darby O'Brien. These three joined pitchers Adonis Terry and Brickyard Kennedy, along with outfielder Oyster Burns and catcher Doc Bushong, a dentist in the offseason. In 1893 Wee Willie Keeler came to Brooklyn following several years of phenomenal hitting with the Baltimore club. Later, pitcher Iron Man Joe McGinnity joined him there.

This 1876 newspaper chronicles the moves of the Mutuals, New York's entry in the newly formed National League. The team was kicked out for refusing to go on costly road trips.

Association, which was the Triple A of its time. The "Brooklyn Ballclub" never really had an official name, but in 1889 everyone called them, of all things, "the Bridegrooms" because six of the players married during the winter. Marriage seems to have agreed with them—in 1889 Brooklyn won the American Association championship.

Colorful early score-cards, including one from Decoration Day 1884 (bottom) when Brooklyn played in the American Associa-tion. The crosstown Giants joined the National League that same year.

The Brooklyn teams in the late 1880s and 1890s were an amalgamation of talent. The owners bought the con-tracts of two stellar pitchers from the St. Louis Browns, Bob Caruthers and Dave Foutz, for $14,250 in 1888. That same year, they signed three players from the American Association's Mets when the franchise folded—first baseman Dave Orr, shortstop Paul Radford, and left

The 1894 Brooklyn Base Ball Club.

An 1890s scorecard (note the ad for $1 shirts).

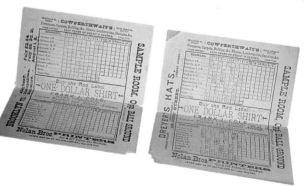

The feisty Byrne, always dreaming of bigger things, promptly challenged the National League champions, the crosstown Giants, to a nine-game "world series"—the forerunner of the October Classic. The series was the first inter-league matchup. But more importantly, it was the first of thousands of heated games between the Giants and the Dodgers that would cross a century and a continent. The more mature, better hitting Giants won the series six games to three, but Brooklyn's ability to play well and draw huge crowds so impressed National League officials that in 1890 the club was asked to join the National League. The

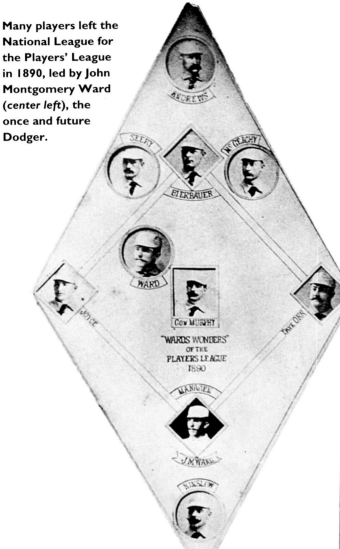

Many players left the National League for the Players' League in 1890, led by John Montgomery Ward (*center left*), the once and future Dodger.

One of the earliest known Dodgers tickets, from 1892.

team that would eventually be called the Dodgers, and that would become a part of American folklore, was born.

In their very first season in the National League in 1890, the Bridegrooms not only had to battle their league rivals but two new competitors in their own backyard. That spring hundreds of players, fed up with what they considered absurdly low wages (sound familiar?), had bolted the National League and the American Association to form their own circuit, the Players' League.

The local players' franchise in Flatbush was the Brooklyn Wonders. The American Association, which had lost the Bridegrooms to the National League, also brought in a new team, the Gladiators, giving Brooklyn three professional teams.

Byrne's Bridegrooms, better paid

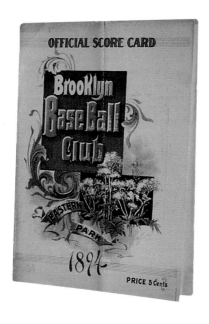

These two score-cards, both sold for a nickel, help trace the Bridegrooms' movements across Brooklyn. The 1890 scorecard (left) is from Washington Park, their first stadium, and the other, dating from 1894, is from Eastern Park. Eastern was built next to trolley tracks, and fans, who had to dodge trolley cars to get to the ballpark, soon started calling each other "Dodgers."

than most, did not desert the team as many National League stars did, and the ball club weathered the storm of the Players' League, which lasted just one year. The loyal players helped Brooklyn win their first National League pennant in 1890 by six and a half games over Chicago.

Flushed with success on the field, if not in the box office, Byrne then built 12,000-seat Eastern Park for his team. The new park was a nice enough idea, but it was located alongside the tracks of the newfangled trolley car, which became an instant menace. The hard-to-control trolleys were so lethal that by the middle of the summer they were killing at least one person a week. One man's entire family

was killed by trolleys that year. The agile, fast-footed fans of the Brooklyn team had to dodge the trolleys to get into Eastern Park and they started to jokingly call each other, and the team, the Dodgers.

Officially, the Dodgers were known as the Bridegrooms for several more years. Then, in 1899, the owners hired manager Ned Hanlon from Baltimore, and he gave Brooklyn a pennant in both of his first two seasons. At the time, a popular if totally unrelated vaudeville act existed known as "Hanlon's Superbas," so the press started calling the team "the Superbas."

Sensing prosperity, in 1901 Ban Johnson, a former sports editor, talked a minor league called the Western Association into joining with some independent clubs to form a new professional league, the American League, to rival the National. The creation of the new league, which was better financed than the American Association and represented more large cities, caused chaos in the National.

Teams that had built loyal followings and profitable box offices since 1876 suddenly had direct competition, and they did not like it. National League teams were also raided by the upstart American League, losing many players to owners with deep pockets.

This time Brooklyn, which had sur-

Right, Charles Ebbets's receipt for the purchase of 190 shares in the Brooklyn Ball Club, February 28, 1899.

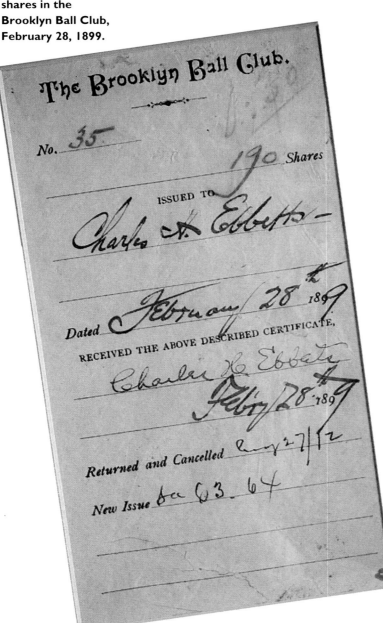

vived the Players' League raids, was hit hard. They lost genuine stars: Fielder Jones, an outfielder, wound up with the White Sox and became their manager. Iron Man Joe McGinnity, who often pitched both ends of a doubleheader and went on to win 35 games in 1904 for the Giants, jumped to the American League's Baltimore team. But the worst loss of all was Wee Willie Keeler, the slight, five-foot, four-inch batting phenomenon who hit at least .338 every year he was with the Dodgers and who jumped to the Yankees.

Punchless, the Dodgers floundered. They stumbled into sixth place in 1904 and fell to last in 1905. In 1907 they lost 16 of their first 17 games and fans expressed concern by pelting players on both sides with soda bottles. Around this time a Dodgers pitcher and catcher were arrested by police in order to stop an illegal Sunday game the Dodgers were playing. And the following season police waded into a Brooklyn stand and arrested three Giants players who were gleefully beating a Dodgers fan to a pulp. Things happened in Brooklyn. Always have.

After Byrne died in 1898 his top assistant, Charlie Ebbets, who had worked his way up from selling programs in the stands, took over. Relying on scouts and rumors, he signed a top amateur pitcher

SUPERBAS — CHIEF MEYERS

SUPERBAS — RUBE MARQUARD

SUPERBAS — OTTO MILLER

SUPERBAS — JAKE DAUBERT

JOE KELLY   FIELDER JONES   NED HANLON *Manager*   JOE McGINNITY   WILLIE KEELER

CHARLES (DUKE) FARRELL   TOM DALY   HUGH JENNINGS   BILL DONOVAN   JIM SHECKARD   BILL DAHLEN

BROOKLYN NATIONAL LEAGUE CHAMPIONS, 1900

Rare individual player pennants from the turn of the century. The flags celebrate a team called neither the Dodgers nor the Bridegrooms but the Superbas. The Dodgers manager then was named Ned Hanlon and a popular vaudeville act of the era was known as Hanlon's Superbas—hence, the team was called the Superbas. It was around this time, 1905 to 1910, that manufacturers first began producing souvenirs like these flags—along with baseball cards, buttons, and hats—to cash in on baseball's booming popularity.

This first-place 1900 team had three Hall of Famers: Willie Keeler (*top right*), Joe McGinnity (*second from right*), and Hugh Jennings (*bottom center*).

named Nap Rucker and a hot-hitting college kid called Zack Wheat. Then someone in Pennsylvania coal country found Jake Daubert, who would star for ten years. But it was in the business office where the young owner made his shrewdest move. Ebbets, a well-dressed, immaculately groomed, slender man with a thick, impressive mustache, bought a piece of land in the middle of nowhere because

23

Dapper Charlie Ebbets started with the Dodgers as a bookkeeper in 1883 and worked his way up to club president by 1898. A man who loved the fans as much as they loved baseball, he invented the rain check so that fans could see all of a ballgame they had paid for and, in 1913, built a new stadium for the Dodgers, named Ebbets Field in a vote by local sportswriters.

he wanted to build a huge new ballpark, one that would house the Dodgers forever.

Wooden parks, people had discovered, were not safe. In 1911, the Giants' first Polo Grounds burned down. Now with a chance to build a coliseum rivaling ancient Rome's, owner John Brush erected the concrete-and-steel Polo Grounds on the Harlem River, a stadium that would last for fifty years. Not to be outdone, Ebbets built Ebbets Field in 1912, a 37,000-seat stadium sitting on four and one-half acres of Brooklyn real estate. Ebbets Field would become to baseball what the Louvre is to art.

This old photo of Ebbets Field shows how it loomed over the neighborhood on the corner of Bedford Avenue and Sullivan Street.

24

One T-206 tobacco card came in each pack of cigarettes. These are part of a vast, 520-card set issued in 1908.

The Federal League was the third major league loop, and, infused with cash from sports-hungry investors, it threatened to crush the National and American leagues. It installed a Brooklyn team called the Tip-Tops (whose owner also held the company that made Tip-Top bread), and added a franchise in Newark (the Peps) that would compete directly with a minor league team there owned by Ebbets. And if all that wasn't bad enough, the Tip-Tops announced that they would soon become the first team to play night baseball. (They would have been, too, but contractors

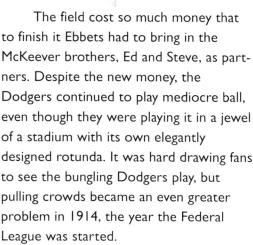

The field cost so much money that to finish it Ebbets had to bring in the McKeever brothers, Ed and Steve, as partners. Despite the new money, the Dodgers continued to play mediocre ball, even though they were playing it in a jewel of a stadium with its own elegantly designed rotunda. It was hard drawing fans to see the bungling Dodgers play, but pulling crowds became an even greater problem in 1914, the year the Federal League was started.

The 1909 Spalding Guide listed the staff of the world champion Brooklyn club.

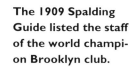

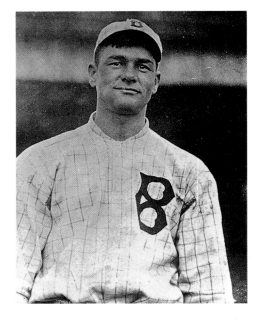

Zack Wheat, who played for Brooklyn from 1909 to 1926, was one of baseball's great hitters. In the dead ball era, he hit 476 doubles, 172 triples, and 132 home runs in compiling a .317 lifetime average. He was elected to the Hall of Fame in 1959.

Brooklyn at spring training in Hot Springs, Arkansas, 1912. The ball club was as ragged-looking here as in the National League, where they finished seventh that year.

never completed their light towers.)

Fortunately for the American and National leagues, Federal finances never worked out and folded after the 1915 season. But Ebbets, in between sleepless nights, had attempted to meet the Tip-Top threat by signing Wilbert Robinson, "Uncle Robbie," as manager in 1914. The huge, burly, affable Uncle Robbie would be manager for eighteen years, a legend in Brooklyn and throughout the game.

Faced with the unenviable task of transforming the Dodgers into a hot property, Robinson hired the talented outfield clown Casey Stengel, nabbed

Above, these 5-inch-high felt souvenirs, created around 1910 and known as "blankets," depict Brooklyn's Nap Rucker and George Cutshaw.

Below, Dodger slugger and Hall of Famer Jake Daubert. Jake, a superb first baseman who came to Brooklyn from the Pennsylvania coal mines, hit .303 lifetime and led the Dodgers to the 1916 Series with a .316 average.

Above, most remember garrulous **Casey Stengel** as the man who took the Yankees to ten pennants in twelve years, but he was quite a ballplayer in his younger days, posting a .284 average in thirteen seasons and .393 in World Series play. He played with the Dodgers from 1913 to 1917, hitting .316 in 1914, and came back to manage the team, unsuccessfully, from 1934 to 1936.

Manager Wilbert "Uncle Robbie" Robinson graced the beautiful cover of the Ebbets Field program for the 1916 Series.

some ex-Federals, and made a few trades. Before long he had strong pitching with Rucker, Jeff Pfeffer, Rube Marquard, and Jack Coombs. Jake Daubert was already one of the league's top hitters and he was joined by John "Chief" Meyers, the Native American catcher whose glory years had been with the Giants. Robinson had Mike Mowrey at third and in the outfield Wheat, Hi Myers, and the colorful Stengel.

The press soon began calling the Brooklyn club the "Robins," short for (Uncle Robbie) Robinson. After a third-place finish in 1915, the team roared into the 1916 season. They started off strong and stayed strong. Two days before the end of the season they clinched their first pennant in 16 years by beating (with great delight) the cross-town Giants, a triumph that qualified them for their first modern-era World Series, against the Boston Red Sox.

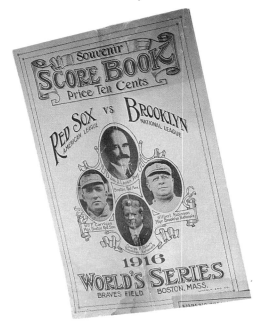

Brooklyn got into its first World Series in 1916, but lost to the Red Sox and a kid pitcher named Babe Ruth.

Thousands of screaming Brooklyn fans lined a parade route from Ebbets Field to Grand Central Station, cheering on their team. Five and six deep in places, they carried large colorful banners, placards, and posters. Some rang cowbells and small boys ran after the open cars as the players rode by. Another 5,000 fans crowded Grand Central Station to give the boys a rousing sendoff as they departed for Boston. It was the borough of Brooklyn's first taste of World Series champagne and the fans were going to savor every drop.

Brooklyn was heady with the Series glow, but the fans who trekked to Boston for the October Classic met their match in the Royal Rooters, the huge and vocal fan club of the Red Sox. The Royal Rooters began the festivities by marching around the stadium through city streets and then marching around the outfield, constantly singing their fight song, "Tessie."

The Red Sox certainly heard them. Although Boston played its Series games at Braves Field because it held more people than Fenway, the strange park did not hurt—the Red Sox took game one, 6-1, as its fans continually broke into new refrains of "Tessie," which drove Brooklyn's Robinson nuts. The Sox then won game two in 14 innings, with the best pitcher in all of baseball, young Babe Ruth (who had 23 wins that year) on the mound.

The five-game series moved back to Brooklyn, where the Robins lost one and won one. Ten thousand fans joined in a snake dance through the outfield at Ebbets after the win. Even though they were down three to one, Brooklyn was delirious. This is what they had been fighting for all these years, since 1900—a shot at the world championship. The Series went back to Boston, though, where the Red Sox wrapped it up with a 4-1 victory in front of 46,620 fans, the largest official crowd yet to see a baseball game. The dream died hard in Canarsie.

Like many pennant winners, the

Boston's Tilly Walker slides safely into third base past Brooklyn's Mike Mowrey in game one of the 1916 World Series against the Dodgers. The Red Sox won the opener, 6-5, and went on to take the Series, four games to one.

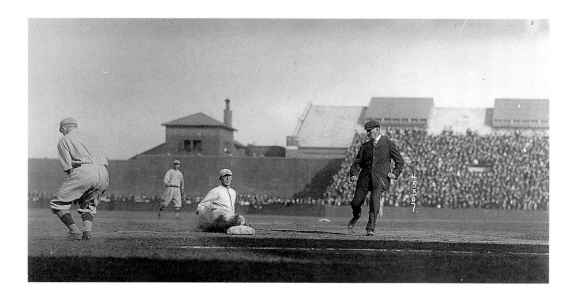

Dodger manager Wilbert Robinson and captain Zack Wheat (left) go over ground rules for the 1920 World Series with Cleveland manager Tris Speaker and umpires.

Two World Series press pins from 1916 and 1920.

Dodgers faded the next season and for many afterward. From 1917 to 1919 the club was in a tailspin. Pitcher Jeff Pfeffer, who won 25 games for the pennant winners in 1916, won only 11 in 1917. Jake Daubert got into a salary dispute, sued Ebbets, and was traded. Several players were drafted when World War I broke out. And, in the biggest loss of all, the irascible Casey Stengel was traded to the Pirates after a salary dispute with Ebbets.

Both the Dodgers dugout and the fans missed Casey, the eternal screwball. He had played well for them, hitting .368 in the last half of the 1914 season and .364 in the 1916 Series. He was an exceptional outfielder, too, one who learned all 112 angles of the Ebbets outfield walls through hundreds of hours of work, and knew every carom of a ball off them.

(Thirty-five years later manager Stengel would teach all of that to Mickey Mantle when the Yanks invaded Ebbets for the 1952 Series.) After leaving the Dodgers, the following season Casey returned to Ebbets as a Pirate and, in one of the stadium's daffiest moments, called time out in his first at-bat, bowed to the crowd, and took his cap off. Out from under it flew a bird! The crowd roared its delight.

By 1920 the lineup had been straightened out, the war was over, and fans and newspapers were calling the Robins the Dodgers, the old-time nickname that had never quite died. Zack Wheat hit over .300 that year and Uncle Robbie added a handful of new players, including pitcher Burleigh Grimes, a spitballer who won 23 games that year, and shortstop Ivy Olson. Fans constantly booed Olson because he made so many errors, so in midseason he took the field with wads of cotton stuffed in his ears.

With its typically colorful and atypically successful 1920 club, the Dodgers picked up another pennant. They then moved on to the World Series, this year against the Cleveland Indians. With classic Dodgers luck, however, the Series was far from the most important event in baseball in 1920. This was the year that Babe Ruth came to the Yankees, crashing a stunning 54 home runs and capturing all the news-

WORLD SERIES PRESS TICKETS, 1920
BROOKLYN NATIONAL LEAGUE BASEBALL CLUB
EBBETS FIELD, BROOKLYN, N. Y.

UPPER TIER

ROW SEC. SEAT

2 K 3

Issued to

Account

President

Treasurer

No. 11

A booklet of press tickets for the ill-fated 1920 World Series issued to *Baseball Magazine*. This was the Series in which Bill Wambsganss pulled off the only unassisted triple play in World Series history against Brooklyn.

paper headlines. This was also the year that Ray Chapman, the Cleveland shortstop, was killed by a pitch, and that baseball had its first commissioner, Kenesaw Mountain Landis. But first and foremost, 1920 was the year of the "Black Sox" scandal at the conclusion of which eight White Sox players indicted for fixing the previous year's World Series were thrown out of baseball forever.

Nevertheless the Dodgers were happy to be in the downplayed Series. At first luck seemed to be with them, and the

Series was tied, two games to two, when game five began. In the fifth inning, with two on and the Dodgers trailing 7-0, Brooklyn pitcher Clarence Miller ripped a line drive toward center. Pete Kilduff on second, thinking it was a single, took off for third, but unheralded Cleveland second baseman Bill Wambsganss leaped into the air, caught the ball, and stepped on the bag, doubling up Kilduff for the second out. Meanwhile Miller had raced past first and was heading toward second when Wambsganss made the catch. Pulling up within six feet of second, Miller was caught and simply stood still as Wambsganss walked two steps and tagged him out for the only unassisted triple play in World Series history.

The Indians went on to win that game, then swept the next two games and won the Series. Everything happened to the Dodgers. It always did.

A rare photo of the only unassisted triple play in World Series history. Bill Wambsganss, Cleveland's second baseman, has just leaped up to catch Dodger Clarence Mitchell's line drive for the first out. His foot touched second as he came down, **doubling up Pete Kilduff (bottom), looking back in disbelief. Otto Miller, who was on first and raced to second, stopped and stood still, totally confused, as Wambsganss reached over and touched him for the third out.**

31

CHAPTER TWO

THE DAFFINESS BOYS
1920–1937

Slugger Babe Herman dug his cleats into the dirt of the batter's box at Ebbets Field and ground his big, meaty hands into the handle of the bat. It was prime time for the mauler. Bases were loaded, nobody was out. Hank DeBerry was on third, pitcher Dazzy Vance on second, Chick Fewster on first, and the prodigious Herman at bat. The fans were stomping their feet. The pitch came in, and Herman hit a tremendous drive toward the right-field wall. It looked like it might be caught by the running right fielder, so DeBerry held up. When it fell and then bounced off the wall, DeBerry trotted home. Vance, on second, did not wait and had rounded third heading home. But out of the corner of his eye he saw the right fielder pick up the ball and, halfway home, decided he couldn't beat the throw; he spun and raced back to third. On first, Fewster was certain the ball was for extra bases from the crack of the bat. He never looked up and kept running the bases, passed second and determined to make third. Herman, convinced he could stretch the hit into a triple, kept his eye on the fielder as he rounded first, then second. Assuming everyone in front of him had scored, Babe charged toward third, still not looking, and slid into the bag—only to find Vance and Fewster standing on it. They were all tagged. Herman had tripled into a double play.

The boys were daffy, all right. Pitcher Burleigh Grimes *(top left)* always wore beard stubble when he pitched, to cover a skin rash; razor blade sales in Brooklyn went down, but so did his ERA. Babe Herman *(top right)* fawned over his son, but once, when he had to leave Ebbets in a hurry to see his wife in the hospital, Herman got so confused that he left the kid at the ballpark. And hurler Boom-Boom Beck *(bottom)* rode out of town shortly after losing 20 games in his rookie debut.

33

It was a typical scene from Ebbets Field in the 1920s and early 1930s, days when the press dubbed the hapless Dodgers "the Daffiness Boys." Everything they did smacked of lunacy and everybody they hired seemed capable of doubling as one of the clowns in the circuses that routinely visited Madison Square Garden. A joke about the 1926 play exemplified the fans' view of their lovably incompetent team:

PASSENGER (overhearing ballgame on cabbie's radio): What's happening in the game?

CABBIE: The Dodgers have three men on base.

PASSENGER: Which base?

Trouble began as soon as they initiated their follow-up pennant campaign in 1921. There was no better time for the Dodgers to return from a World Series appearance and prepare to take a second straight pennant than the start of the Roaring Twenties, when all of New York City roared along with its people. Life was never more boisterous or hopeful in the borough of Brooklyn. The city and national economies were booming and jobs were plentiful. Nightlife sparkled with more Broadway shows running than at any time in history and the "talkies" were about to debut. Brooklyn, like Manhattan, was dotted with hundreds of illegal

Babe Herman's slapstick exploits (Dazzy Vance called him "the headless horseman of Ebbets Field") overshadowed his prodigious hitting. Herman averaged .324 lifetime and in 1930 he hit .393, still a Dodger record.

A Dodgerette Fan Club button stuck into a Twenties cap.

speakeasies for people with a wet whistle during Prohibition. Young people in Brooklyn dance halls wobbled all night long to the dance sweeping the nation, the Charleston. In the summer there were two places where it seemed like everybody in Brooklyn went. One was Coney Island, with its legendary amusement parks and wide, pristine beaches jammed with bathers. The other was Ebbets Field.

Above, the 1920s saw the beginnings of baseball cards issued in candy packs, like these American Caramel cards. Jake Daubert, who had played for the Dodgers for nine years, had been traded to Cincinnati shortly before the cards were made.

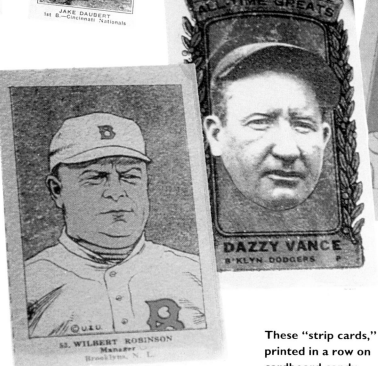

These "strip cards," printed in a row on cardboard candy boxes and then cut up, were issued in the mid-Twenties. Uncle Robbie and Dazzy Vance cards are particularly valuable.

35

Dazzy Vance wasn't brought up to the majors until he was 28, but he made up for lost time, striking out 2,045 batters in 13 years, leading the league in strike-outs seven years in a row, and winning 197 games.

But there was no joy in Ebbets in 1921. In just a single meteoric year, the mighty Dodgers plummeted from first to fifth in the National League and they stayed there. Nobody could explain it. A team that won the pennant in 1916 and 1920 had mysteriously collapsed right in front of the fans' eyes. It wasn't the manager. Wilbert Robinson, good old Uncle Robbie, was as clever in 1921 as he had been in 1920. The Dodgers' top hitter, Zack Wheat, had another fine year. In fact, in just about every year during the Twenties and Thirties, the Dodgers' roster included .300 hitters.

The team had two of the best pitchers in baseball in Burleigh Grimes and Dazzy Vance. Grimes was a rugged, consistent pitcher, one of those hurlers no one pays much attention to until the end of the season when he wins his twentieth game. He was a rock-solid anchor for the Dodgers from 1918 to 1926, winning at least twenty games for them in four different seasons (and 270 lifetime). In his final year with the Dodgers he triumphed in just 12, but went on to win 19 the next season for the Giants. Grimes was so good that he later won 25 in a season for Pittsburgh. He was menacing, too, with a rare skin condition that caused his face to turn bright red in the heat. To camouflage it, Burleigh always wore a two-day stubble of beard. Batters looking out at him saw a tawdry looking buccaneer with a fastball.

The tall, lean Dazzy Vance was just as good as Grimes. The geniuses in the Dodgers farm system had forced the hard-throwing Vance to remain in their minor league system for ten long years before they brought him up in 1922, a 31-year-old rookie. He also underwent an arm operation, and his new arm, plus a better schedule for rest, enabled him to bloom immediately.

Vance had a strange, rear-back-and-chuck style of pitching that threw most hitters off their timing. He led the

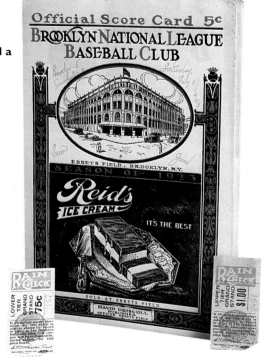

Ticket stubs and a scorecard from the mid-1920s.

week. Once, blinded by the Coney Island sun, he was hit on the head with a fly ball. Another time he was accused of putting an entire lighted cigar in his mouth ("only the tip was lighted," he argued), and on yet another occasion, rushing to see his wife in the hospital after a game, he forgot his son and left him at the ballpark.

Herman epitomized the Daffiness Boys, but there were many others.

Consider the mercurial pitcher Boom-Boom Beck. Walter Beck came to the team in 1933 and without even warming up proceeded to lose 20 games. Basketball teams had lower ERAs than Boom-Boom (the first "boom" of his nick-

National League in strikeouts seven times in the 1920s. In 1924 he won 28 games (with a 2.16 ERA) and received an MVP award. He continued pitching in the majors until he was 44 years old.

Vance and Grimes would have been great stoppers for any team, but they didn't help the Dodgers much. When it came to the Daffiness Boys everyone from the front office to the far reaches of the center-field bleachers just thought they'd lost it. No one symbolized that like Herman, the lovable, huge, blond-haired, blue-eyed behemoth. His three-men-on-a-base stunt was just one in a long line of mishaps. The Babe was passed on the bases by his own teammates two different times in a single

Boom-Boom Beck started off his Dodger career by losing 20 games in his first season, He had only two winning seasons (one with a 1-0 mark) in the majors.

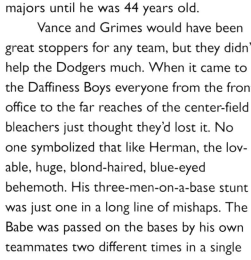

37

People loved the name of pitcher Van Lingle Mungo so much that someone even wrote a song about him.

name came from the ball hitting the bat, the second from the ball hitting the outfield wall). One day in Philadelphia, Beck was removed from the game (a common occurrence) and was so angry that he hurled the ball into right field and sent it crashing into the wall. Dodgers right fielder Hack Wilson, chatting with fans while the pitching change was made, assumed that the new pitcher had come in and the game had been resumed while he was not paying attention. He raced after the ball and threw it to second base. The manager winced.

And then there was Van Lingle Mungo in the Thirties, actually a pretty good pitcher whom nobody appreciated

Player rosters from the 1930s.

because they spent so much time mutilating his name. Mungo's name so fascinated people that someone even wrote a song about him. Journeyman pitcher Dutch Leonard also played for the Dodgers, doing all the right things as the men behind him did all the wrong things. Another intriguing hurler was Clyde "Pea Ridge" Day, who hailed, of course, from Pea Ridge, Arkansas. Day was a veteran hog caller back home and would howl "soooooeeeyyyy" after strikeouts.

Also on the roster of Dodgers eccentrics was Buddy Hassett, an efficient hitter who was even better at singing Irish

EBBETS FIELD

Fans flock to Ebbets Field in the spring of 1913 when it first opened. At the time it was considered too large for a major league ballpark, but in the end the Dodgers left because it was too small.

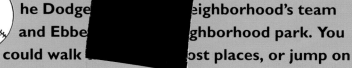

The Dodge[...] eighborhood's team and Ebbe[...] ghborhood park. You could walk [...] ost places, or jump on a train and ride five minutes. You were safe there. You felt comfortable. It was home away from home. A guy with two little kids who had to buy a beer would just turn to the guy next to him and ask him to keep an eye on the kids while he was gone. Would you do that today? It was one big family. Whenever I went to Ebbets I thought it was the greatest place in the world.

—AL PANASUK, FAN, MADISON, NEW JERSEY

EBBETS FIELD

Every time I'd kneel in the on-deck circle this guy in the first row of seats would start talking to me. We'd have nice little conversations three or four times a game—whenever I was up—and we got to be friends. You were so close to the seats that you'd talk in conversational tones. It was king of amazing. It gave you a feel for the people—you knew them.

—CAL ABRAMS, Dodgers

This pin commemorates Ebbets Field from 1913, when it opened, to 1957, when the team left for California.

You've heard of the twelfth man in football, the crowd? The Dodgers had 35,000 extra men in Ebbets. The fan support gave them the edge in every single game.

—TV STAR CHUCK CONNORS,
WHO PLAYED BRIEFLY FOR THE DODGERS

232.—EBBET'S FIELD, BROOKLYN, N.Y.

Above, this 1920s postcard is a gorgeous drawing of Ebbets.

Right, fifty seasons of Dodgers signed this commemorative Ebbets plate.

My father, he worried a lot about business, but when he took me to Ebbets Field he was another person. He'd sit there in the sunshine and smile and laugh. That's how I like to remember him, smiling at the ball game in Brooklyn.

—MARJORIE DAUMAN, FAN, NEW YORK CITY

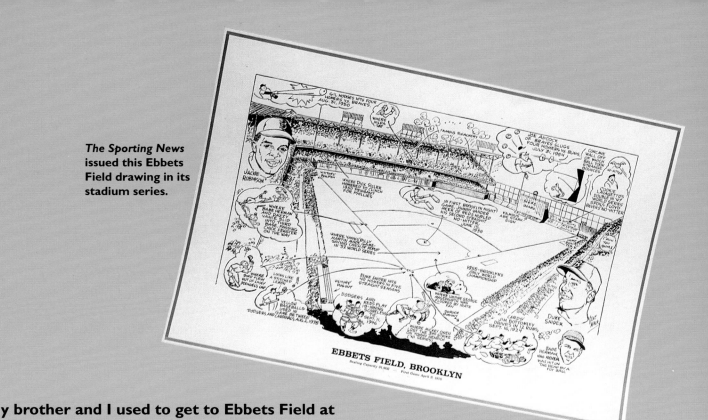

The Sporting News issued this Ebbets Field drawing in its stadium series.

My brother and I used to get to Ebbets Field at 9 a.m., when the gates opened, for a 1 p.m. game. We'd bring an old brown bag full of peanut butter and jelly sandwiches our mother made for the day—must have been ten for each of us. We'd watch pitchers warm up, outfielders jog, the maintenance people water the field, the ushers seat people. Anything. We just had to be there, if to do nothing more than smell that wonderful grass and listen to people talk as they walked along Bedford Avenue. We'd stay until the end of the game—nobody left games early in Brooklyn—and then walk home. We'd get home at 4:30 or so and spend the rest of the night talking about the game. You just didn't go to a game then—it was a special event, an all-day affair.

—JACK PRATHER, FAN, LAKE TRANQUILITY, NEW JERSEY

This snappy cap belonged to one of the ushers at Ebbets Field.

Above, a season pass from 1929.

I had box seats at Ebbets for years. People told me I was the greatest baseball fan they ever met. They were wrong. I was never a fan of baseball. I was a fan of the Brooklyn Dodgers. There's a big difference.

I loved them for everything and I loved them completely. Ebbets Field . . . that was a fantasy park, a neighborhood park for one and all. And those names! Cam-pan-ell-a, Newk, Oisk, Van Lingle Mungo, Whit-low Wyatt, Coo-kie Lav-a-gett-o, Boom-Boom Beck. Why, they just roll off your tongue. And we always laughed about the kings in Europe. Who needs kings when the Dodgers had the Duke?

—COMIC ALAN KING, FAN, NEW YORK

folk songs. He entertained the team, win or lose, in the locker room after games with many-versed renditions of "My Wild Irish Rose." And then there was the Dodgers' very own lord, Lord Jimmy Jordan, the first and only member of the royalty to play baseball in America (Duke Snider doesn't count). Jordan went from the infield to a lordship when he married a member of the British royalty.

Even the announcers were daffy. The team's public address man, Tex Rickart, was famous for malapropisms that make Ralph Kiner look like the editor-in-chief of Webster's. Rickart once intoned sonorously, "A little boy has been found lost," and on another occasion, spotting shirts hanging on an outfield fence, he warned fans, "Will the fans along the out-field railing please remove their clothes."

In 1925 Charlie Ebbets died, and the Dodgers' situation continued to deterio-rate. Ebbets had been the brains behind the team and its backbone (he worked for the Dodgers all of his life), and thousands attended his rain-soaked funeral. The funeral cortege drove past Ebbets Field on its way to the cemetery, where the owner was buried a few yards from Henry Chadwick, who invented the scoring sys-tem. But Ed McKeever, Ebbets's partner, caught pneumonia in the rain and died a week later. McKeever's brother, Steve, took over the team. Determined to bring the Dodgers back to 1920 World Series form, he ran them right into the ground, trading away Zack Wheat, hard-hitting Jack Fournier, and, later, Babe Herman. Despite his troubles running bases and fielding, Babe was a fan favorite and a tremendous hitter, batting .393 in 1930 and .324 lifetime. Fans were enraged. For no apparent reason, in 1933 the front office then traded away Watty Clark, a twenty-game winner.

The death of Ebbets seemed to be a turning point, but sadly for the worse. Or maybe it was the time Dazzy Vance threw a one-hitter and could only win 1-0. Or maybe it was the time Alex Ferguson had to be brought in as a relief pitcher in the very first inning, and on top of that the Dodgers' infield made four errors. Or maybe it was the day Herman was taken out of the game for dropping yet another fly ball and was replaced by Alta Cohen, an energetic rookie who got so caught up in his debut that instead of batting ninth, where he was supposed to hit, he batted third without anyone realizing it.

The team's owners were constantly trying to put together winning combinations on the field, but they did nothing right and ended the 1930s by buying and trading for a bunch of fading superstars. Dave Bancroft (age 38), Lefty O'Doul (34), Waite Hoyt (32), and Hack Wilson (33) had little left but their reputations, so when that strategy failed, the owners hired and fired managers. Robinson was

A late Twenties pennant.

Lefty O'Doul, like many others, spent his twilight years with the Dodgers in the Thirties. This button commemorated his 1932 batting title

Left, Dodger memorabilia from Brooklyn's finest years.

Below, Wilbert Robinson *(right)* with John McGraw in Uncle Robby's rookie season as Dodger skipper. He would take the

Dodgers to two pennants while assembling a roster of cast-offs and odd-balls. Robinson was as much a character as his players. Once he agreed to catch a baseball dropped from an airplane, but a player on the plane dropped a

grapefruit instead, which exploded as Robinson caught it.

Right, in the race until the very end, Brooklyn printed up these tickets for the 1930 World Series but never made it, finishing six games out.

booted in 1932 and replaced with Max Carey, a fine player who left in two years. Popular player Casey Stengel, the first man to hit an inside-the-park home run in a World Series, took over the team in 1934 and was gone after three summers. The men at the helm contributed to the daffy image of the Dodgers, especially Casey. One day, with the Dodgers ahead of the Giants, he was trying his hardest to get the game called due to rain so it would go into the books as a win. The umpires wouldn't do it, so the next time the Giants were up, the Ol' Perfessor put on a pair of loud striped socks, pulled a huge umbrella off the bench, and marched out to coach third base. He raised his feet up and down as if wading in a deep pud-dle and twirled his umbrella over his head; the home plate umpire, furious, threw him out of the game. Another time when Casey was given a press photo clearly showing the Giants' Mel Ott out by two feet in the previous day's game, although the ump called him safe, Casey marched out to home and pinned it right on the plate.

Above, this fiftieth anniversary bat, manufactured in 1933, honored Brooklyn's first pro team, from 1883, some of whose members pose in the picture. Considering that the 1933 club finished 26 1/2 games out of first, maybe they should have put some of these guys in the lineup.

Above right, a season pass from 1936.

were thriving. The Dodgers and Giants were parties in a great rivalry that thrilled New York from 1890 to 1957, but it was the Giants who dominated the National League. John McGraw's boys won ten pennants from 1900 to 1925, and in the Thirties they won three more. The Giants had the country's most noted manager in the irascible McGraw and the country's best pitchers first in Christy Mathewson ▮▮▮▮ in Carl Hubbell during the ▮▮▮▮ The Giants had a fearsome lineup ▮▮▮ that included Bill Terry, Frankie ▮▮▮ Ott, Roger Bresnahan, and ▮▮▮ets Kelly. While the Dodgers ▮▮▮ collar Raggedy Anns all the way, ▮▮▮ were a glamour club, with the ▮▮▮ollege-educated Mathewson, ▮▮▮dressed Terry, and night owl

▮▮▮ if that wasn't bad enough, the ▮▮▮espised Yankees emerged as a ▮▮▮ in the early Twenties with the arrival of Babe Ruth. They tore up the American League for the next 20 years, grabbing all the headlines that should have been reserved for the Dodgers. The Yanks were so good that they needed a mammoth, 67,000-seat stadium built in 1923 to house all their fans. The lowly Dodgers, the Daffiness Boys, were third in records, third in stadiums, and third in recognition, the poor cousins across the East River.

At first the Dodgers' lack of success did not bother the loyal fans, who saw the Daffiness Boys as quaint and lovable. Right up to 1930, the team drew close to a million fans a year. But what began to dismay the faithful was the woeful state of the Dodgers, year after year, in the very same decades that the hated Giants and Yankees

One of the hundreds of "Brooklyn Bum" cartoons drawn by newspaper illustrator Willard Mullins. The down-and-out Bum, created in the 1930s, was a symbol of the Dodgers' ineptitude. Ironically, fans not only embraced him, but used Mullins' Bum as their symbol of success in the Forties and Fifties.

D'YEZ MEAN I WASN'T REALLY BORNDED IN BROOKLYN ATALL?

These late Thirties cards were fan favorites.

"WHIT" WYATT

KIRBY HIGBE

"DOLPH" CAMILLI

By the end of the Thirties, the Dodgers had fallen into disrepair on all fronts. Between 1921 and 1937 the team finished sixth of eight eleven times and seventh once. And finally the fans, loyal for so long, began to abandon them. While the Giants and Yankees continued to pull large crowds, the average attendance at Ebbets (as high as 20,000 per game in 1930), slipped to a skimpy 6,300 in 1937. Barnstorming black teams such as the Brooklyn Royal Giants, the Lincoln Giants, and the Homestead Grays, which rented Ebbets for doubleheaders, pulled 15,000. Even the local borough semipro team, the Bushwicks, drew 12,000 on Sundays at nearby Dexter Park.

Everybody outdrew the Dodgers. The press was pounding them regularly and illustrator Willard Mullins of the *New York World Telegraph* made them out to be national buffoons with his famous "Bums" cartoons. The club had not turned a profit since 1930, and by 1937 the team owed the Brooklyn Trust Company half a million dollars. Physically, old Ebbets Field was falling apart. The Dodgers were dying.

THE NEW DODGERS
1938–1946

r. Leland MacPhail never did things the way people expected. He received his college degree after racing through three colleges in three years, paying his way by playing professional baseball in the summers under an assumed name. Later, as general manager of the Cincinnati Reds, he became the very first executive to introduce night baseball to the major leagues. Larry MacPhail was impatient and strong-minded, and everything he did had the same character. Who better to make a wild attempt to turn the nearly bankrupt and failing Brooklyn Dodgers around?

Brought to New York in 1938, the 47-year-old general manager was given the job of making winners out of losers, outdrawing the Giants and Yankees, rebuilding Ebbets Field, and changing the Dodgers' image as baseball's baffled bums. MacPhail tore into his work. In his very first year he put in lights at Ebbets and introduced night baseball to Brooklyn, giving attendance a big boost. He hired radio announcer Red Barber and made the Dodgers the first team to broadcast their games live. Barber's voice became the voice of summer on the streets of Brooklyn. It was like music, and you heard it everywhere you went—candy stores, gas stations, laundromats. MacPhail hired Babe Ruth as a coach to build up the gate, and he took his feisty shortstop, Leo Durocher, and made

"Beat the Yanks" was all anyone could think about in this September 29, 1941, parade to celebrate the Dodgers' first pennant in fully 21 years. MacPhail and Durocher sit together in back of the parade's lead car.

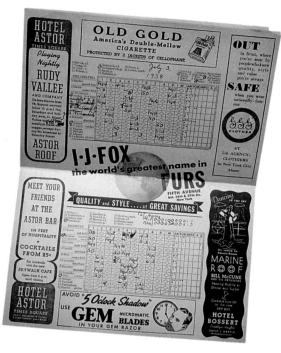

A 1938 scorecard
from a game against
the Phillies in which
Cookie Lavagetto
went one for three.

Brand new general
manager Leland
("Larry") MacPhail
(left), seen here with
manager Burleigh
Grimes at spring
training in 1938, was
hired away from the
Reds and would turn
Brooklyn fortunes
upside down.

Right, Ruth auto-
graphed the center
ball, a team ball
from the 1938 club,
as well as that on
the left. The older
ball on right was
signed by Uncle
Robbie in the late
Twenties.

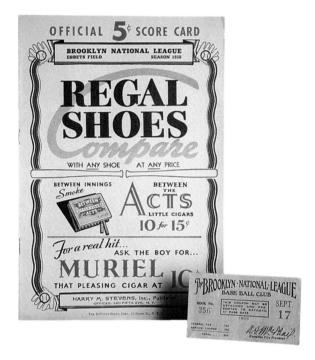

A 1938 score-card and ticket coupon.

The Dodgers hired Ruth to hawk the team and used his image on everything they could find, including this exhibition game scorecard from 1938. At right, another ornate opening-day ticket, 1939.

him the manager. In addition, workers completely renovated crumbling Ebbets.

In his office high above Ebbets Field, MacPhail performed some impressive sleight-of-hand tricks in trading and hiring players. A veteran baseball man who had worked wonders with the Reds, MacPhail signed Dolph Camilli, Dixie Walker, Pee Wee Reese, and Pistol Pete Reiser. He cleaned house and either traded or retired all of the Daffiness Boys.

MacPhail was strictly business. The all-new Dodgers thundered into third place in 1939, second in 1940, and, miraculously, first in 1941. The Dodgers dominated the newspapers, the radio, and for the first time the National League. Fans who loved the team but just couldn't handle two decades of failure returned to Ebbets in hordes, dodging every trolley in the neighborhood. In MacPhail's first year, the team drew 955,000 fans to its bright, clean, newly refurbished park, double the total for 1937. Radio coverage of the team only helped to pull more people to the ballpark to see games in person. Night games, designed for the fan who worked all day, were a huge success. In the very first Ebbets night game, 38,748 fans jammed the ballpark under the lights to see history as Reds pitcher Johnny Vander Meer hurled his second consecutive no-hitter (a feat never matched). "I was so

MacPhail was responsible for innovative and ornate opening-day tickets.

These Playball cards from 1939 honored many Dodgers.

hot that week that it didn't make any difference if I was pitching at night or in the daytime. I just could do no wrong," laughed the Reds' Vander Meer years later.

It was at the plate that the all-new Dodgers excelled. MacPhail had spared no expense in buying ballplayers and no egos in trading them. Backed by the owners and even the Brooklyn Trust Company,

LOWER STAND
19 8 9
SEC ROW SEAT

Opening Day
EBBETS FIELD

BROOKLYN
DODGERS
· 1940 ·

EST. PRICE $1.50
FED. TAX .15
Total $1.65

RAIN CHECK
Not Redeemable for Cash

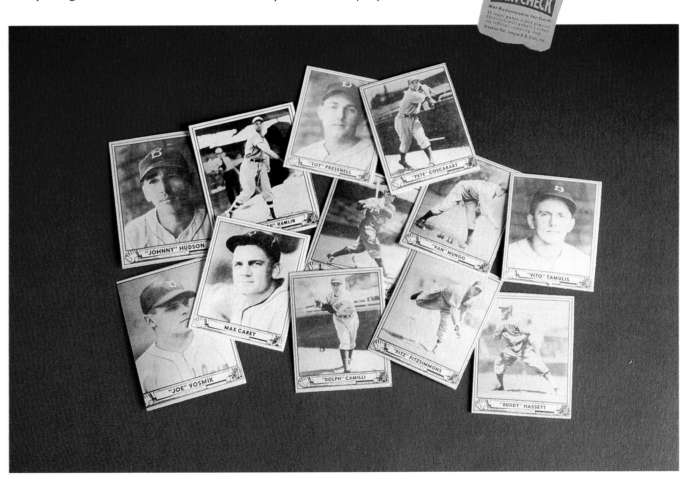

"TOT" PRESSNELL · "PETE" COSCARART · "JOHNNY" HUDSON · "VAN" MUNGO · "VITO" TAMULIS · MAX CAREY · "JOE" VOSMIK · "DOLPH" CAMILLI · "FITZ" FITZSIMMONS · "BUDDY" HASSETT

Brooklyn Dodgers • Ebbets Field

Opening Day 1941

Est. Price $1.50
Fed. Tax .15
TOTAL $1.65

LOWER STAND
14 **15** **15**
SEC. ROW SEAT
Brooklyn National League Baseball Club, Inc.

R. W. McPhail
PRESIDENT

◄ **RAIN CHECK** ►

Not Redeemable for Cash
If legal game is not played this stub will
admit bearer on official opening day.
Brooklyn National League Baseball Club, Inc.

Above, a familiar sight—Leo Durocher arguing with an umpire. Here, in the 1941 World Series, he chews out plate ump Bill McGowan as pitcher Whitlow Wyatt chimes in. Leo took the Dodgers to the Series in just his third year at the helm.

Left, another of MacPhail's lovely opening-day cards from 1941.

MacPhail had traveled to every major- and minor-league ballpark in search of talent, and when he found it, he bought it.

Destiny sat in Ebbets Field in the spring and summer of 1941 (she sat in the bleachers out in center, of course). MacPhail continued to make moves, trades, and then more of both. First came Billy Herman. The sharp-fielding second baseman had been a star with the Chicago Cubs for nine seasons, playing in a number of All Star games and on three pennant winners. A .304 lifetime hitter, he averaged .291 in 1941, the year he was traded to the Dodgers, and .330 in 1943. Herman was a classic number-two hitter and a hit and run specialist who fit perfectly into management's plans.

MacPhail then helped player-manager Durocher rearrange the Dodgers' already explosive team. Pistol Pete Reiser, one of the most gifted hitters in history, was moved from third to center. During his first year with the Dodgers, 1940, he batted .293 in 58 games, but the next season he exploded for a league-leading .343 average. The aggressive Reiser's career began to fade in 1942, however, after he ran into an outfield wall and was injured. In fact Reiser would run into ten more walls in his career, once hurting himself so badly

53

Above, the 1941 Dodgers lineup at the start of the World Series.

Right, the ball closest has the John Hancocks of Leo Durocher and Joe "Ducky" Medwick, reunited on the Dodgers after their years with the Gashouse Gang in St. Louis. Catcher Gus Mancuso signed the ball at right.

that he was given last rites. Reiser's injuries made baseball develop a warning track for outfielders and install padded walls.

When it came to reorganizing the team, MacPhail stumbled by benching the popular, blond-haired Dixie Walker, a.k.a. "the People's Cherce." Dixie had hit .308 in 1940, but he was moved to make way for MacPhail's latest acquisition, Paul Waner. Fans roared their disapproval at every game and Walker was returned to the outfield, where he hit a hefty .311 in 1941. He remained a star for most of the Forties, hitting a league-leading .357 in 1944 and heading up the league's RBIs in 1945 with 124. Opposed to hiring black ballplayers at first, Dixie, a Southerner, soon took a liking to Jackie Robinson and wound up giving him hitting pointers.

As for his other players, MacPhail stuck Ducky Medwick, a prominent prankster with the St. Louis Gashouse Gang in the 1930s, out in left field. Cookie Lavagetto went to third, and Pee Wee Reese became the shortstop. Actually, MacPhail was opposed to Reese, whose skills he held in low regard, but Durocher insisted that the baby-faced ballplayer stay in the lineup. The manager's hunch paid off big time—Reese would become one of the best and most beloved Dodgers, and wound up in the Hall of Fame. Although he was only a .269 lifetime hitter, he was an exceptional fielder who made seven All Star teams. But Reese was a leader above all else, and his teammates cherished him for that. He was named captain soon after he arrived in Brooklyn and many credit his deep friendship with Jackie Robinson as the reason so many fans accepted Robinson when he came up.

MacPhail didn't touch Dolph Camilli, a man born to play first like Lee Iacocca was born to sell cars. In addition, Camilli was no slouch with a bat, hitting more than 23 home runs eight seasons in a row. In 1941 he hit 34 homers and 120 RBIs and was voted the National League's MVP. The year after the 1942 Dodgers-Yankees World Series, Camilli's record slumped to .252 followed by .246 in 1943, but fans were stunned when Camilli was traded—

Dolph Camilli, obtained from the Phillies in 1938 for Larry MacPhail's "new" Dodgers, hit 23 or more homers eight straight years. He was one of the most popular Dodgers of the era, a player who loved the fans as much as they loved him. Traded to the Giants in 1943, he was so upset he refused to go and retired instead.

died in St. Paul, but he somehow managed to develop an exceedingly slow and torturous curve ball that gave him new life. His record with Brooklyn was a solid 8-3 in 1939 and a passable 15-14 in 1940. In 1941, though, Wyatt experienced one of those splendid summers that fans marvel about. Throwing in a trance, the washed-up old pitcher managed to win a staggering 22 games for the Dodgers. He not only won games, he won the big ones. In late September Wyatt claimed a 1-0 thriller over St. Louis that held off the charging Cardinals, and then clinched the

This Dodger doll celebrates the second-place finish of the club in 1940.

Right, the "washed-up" pitcher Whitlow Wyatt won 22 games and the pennant clincher for the Bums in 1941.

to the Giants, no less. Rather than report to the hated Giants, he retired from baseball.

Finally, a touch of inspiration came from good old Whitlow Wyatt, out there in the bullpen. The has-been pitcher with the big windup and kick had been picked up on a whim from a minor league club in St. Paul, Minnesota, which was about to retire him in 1938. Wyatt's fastball had

Thousands of Dodgers fans camped out the night before the first game of the 1941 World Series to buy $1.10 bleacher seats at Ebbets.

pennant for the Bums with a 6-0 shutout over the Braves.

Wyatt was just one more element in the marvelous chemistry in the 1941 Dodgers club. Brooklyn fans saw this as the start of a dynasty that would rival the Yankees of the Twenties and the Giants at the turn of the century. They had the players, they had the moment, and they had good old Whitlow Wyatt, going through his second life. But history was cruel in an odd way to the Dodgers. The tragic loss of the 1941 World Series to the Yankees somehow labeled the Dodgers as the great team that just couldn't win the world championship, the Bums who, no matter how many games they won, just couldn't pick up the big prize. Instead of hating them for it, the fans loved them. The 1941 season started the chapter that made the Dodgers an American institution.

This was the first Dodger-Yankee subway series, and the red-hot Dodgers had the momentum. The Yankees won the first game, the Dodgers the second, and the Yanks the third. The Dodgers played well throughout, and when game four came up, victory seemed certain. But then the unbelievable happened the way it always did to the Bums of Brooklyn.

With two out in the ninth inning, the Dodgers held a 4-3 lead. Pitcher Hugh Casey nailed a 3-2 count on batter Tommy

Henrich. When Casey threw a big-breaking curve ball, Henrich swung and missed. Game over. Series tied. But wait . . . catcher Mickey Owen missed the ball! It fell under his glove and rolled. Henrich, startled, scampered to first. DiMaggio singled, Charlie Keller doubled, and before the inning was over the Yankees held a 7-4 lead. They would win the game and build up a three-games-to-one lead. The next day they won the World Series over the totally deflated Dodgers.

57

This is the glove catcher Mickey Owen was wearing when he failed to catch the legendary third strike on Tommy Henrich that enabled the Yanks to win game four.

The loss was painful, but the Series was the start of something big. Perhaps the venerable *Brooklyn Eagle* said it best in their headline after the final game: "Wait Till Next Year." For a decade and a half more it would always be next year for the Dodgers, but every next year would be exciting, and in every next year the Dodgers would come oh-so-close.

In 1942 the Yankees again won the pennant, which was becoming habitual during those years. And the Dodgers blew the pennant, which was also becoming habitual. This time the Brooklyn boys ran off to a hefty 10½-game lead and then

The 1941 Series seemed in the bag until Dodger catcher Mickey Owen dropped this third strike on the Yankees' Tommy Henrich in the sixth game. The Bombers went on to win the game and the Series.

folded in face of the Cardinals, who then beat the Bronx Bombers in the Series. The Dodgers also suffered a great loss that season when Pistol Pete Reiser, a genuine superstar, ran into the concrete center-field wall in midseason, suffering a concussion. He finished the season, but a great talent was wrecked.

America's entry into World War II saw an exodus of ballplayers into the service. It seemed that every star on the horizon was boarding a troop ship—even stars like Joe DiMaggio and Ted Williams. The Dodgers not only lost Rex Barney, Hugh Casey, Billy Herman, Al Campanis,

Hilda Chester, the fabled leather-lunged fan from Ebbets, traveled to Bear Mountain, N.Y., to lead fans at an exhibition game in 1943. "You might have trouble hearing the PA system at the ballpark, but you never had trouble hearing Hilda," remembered pitcher Ralph Branca.

This 1940s Old Timers Day game was one of the first in baseball.

Jackie Robinson, with Branch Rickey, signs his 1948 contract, reportedly for $14,000. Robinson was named Rookie of the Year and led the Dodgers to the World Series in 1947, the year he broke baseball's sad color line.

Pete Reiser, Gene Hermanski, Cookie Lavagetto, and Pee Wee Reese to the military, but at the end of 1942 General Manager MacPhail enlisted, too. The club replaced MacPhail with the workhorse vice president of the St. Louis Cardinals, Branch Rickey, a stylish dresser with an endless collection of bow ties and an even bigger collection of cigars. Rickey, an eloquent and persuasive talker, had developed the Cardinals' productive farm system (65 of his young charges eventually played for the parent club) and was determined to do the same for the Dodgers. He was convinced that if the Dodgers

could develop young talent during the war, they could be the dominant team in the National League after it.

At first Rickey had to work with Band-Aids. Decimated by the war, all major league teams hired old-timers or young players with little experience, some just out of high school. The Dodgers put together a patchwork wartime team that almost won a pennant in 1942, but the Cardinals beat them, winning 106 games in the process. The next year the team slipped to third and plunged to seventh in 1944. The summer the war ended they sneaked back up to third.

The peace treaties with Germany and Japan signaled a new era for the Dodgers. It was time, finally, for Branch Rickey to unveil the graduates of his farm system. It was also time to unveil another of Rickey's ideas, one that would change the face of baseball and America forever.

There had been three great major league baseball teams in St. Louis in 1914, the year Branch Rickey managed the St. Louis Browns: the Cardinals, the Browns, and the Stars. Everybody in the country knew about the Cardinals and the Browns, and everybody in St. Louis knew about the Stars, an all-black team that barnstormed through the area, playing black and sometimes white teams. The Stars played many of their games on Sunday afternoons, and although the mainstream white press ignored them about 20 percent of their fans were white. Branch Rickey was one of the fans who sat in wooden grandstands watching the Stars play great baseball. And he shook his head each time he saw a great black ballplayer he could not sign because of segregation in the major leagues.

Rickey went on to serve as an executive with the Browns and later the Cardinals through the 1920s and '30s. In those days the St. Louis–Kansas City–Chicago area was a mecca of black baseball. Rickey watched some of the strongest clubs in the Negro Leagues, including the Kansas City Monarchs, with the sensational Satchel Paige. He saw the Chicago American Giants and kept up with the black All-Star game held in Chicago each summer from 1933 on. When he moved to Brooklyn in 1942 to take over the Dodgers, he became familiar with the black teams that played in Ebbets Field and in nearby Brooklyn and Queens ballparks, drawing crowds often larger than the Dodgers'. He watched these extraordinary clubs with envy and, as a major league general manager, with frustration.

Like so many owners and executives,

Rickey knew that the top black ballplayers were just as good as the top white players in the major leagues. If he could sign four or five of the Negro League stars, the Dodger GM knew he could build an invincible ball club in Brooklyn. He also knew that the fans of Brooklyn had seen and appreciated black professional teams from 1852, when the first all-black teams played there. Five pro black teams—the Brooklyn Royal Giants, Lincoln Stars, Harlem Stars, Black Yankees, and Cuban Stars—consistently drew crowds of 10,000 or more to games in New York from 1915 through 1942. All-black doubleheaders in Yankee Stadium drew

Jackie Robinson signed the sweet spot on this Forties team ball.

25,000. If any fans were amenable to a challenge to the color line, it was the people of Brooklyn.

In 1946, Rickey, a lone crusader for integration, made his move and did the unthinkable—he signed a black ballplayer to a major league contract, an athlete named Jackie Robinson.

Branch Rickey's pioneering efforts won no praise in the owners' offices high atop the country's major league stadiums.

Rickey may have seen a rainbow future but the other owners saw one color and one color only—white. Every single owner had voted against the signing of Robinson. Frustrated and depressed, Rickey had turned to baseball's new commissioner, Hap Chandler, who could override the vote. And Chandler, whose job depended on the approval of all the owners, backed Rickey.

"All he was doing was signing a

Jackie Robinson stealing home one of 19 times in his career, including once in the 1955 World Series. Robinson, one of the game's fastest runners, stole 197 bases lifetime in an era when stealing was not encouraged by managers.

Buttons of Whitlow Wyatt and Dolph Camilli, two of the Boys of Summer, with Roger Kahn's classic of the same name.

ballplayer," said Chandler. "If he wants Jackie Robinson, that's his business."

And so three men, a shortstop from a Negro League ballclub, a transplanted midwesterner, and a rookie baseball commissioner, gently shoved open the door to integration.

Jackie Robinson was a UCLA All-American football star who had played a year of Negro League baseball and put in four years with the Army. He was well educated, talented, and used to discipline. And he was tough. Nobody, black or white, was going to push him around. Jackie Robinson loved to win and hated to lose. There was a long meeting in Rickey's office during which Rickey told him every single epithet he would be called, of which "nigger" was the kindest. Robinson would have to take it, and on top of all that, he would have to play sensationally.

Jackie's introduction to white baseball was nasty. He arrived at the Dodgers' Montreal minor league team for 1946 spring-training camp, which they shared with the Dodgers, after having been asked to get off two different buses and spending a night in a "colored-only" bus waiting room. At spring training, one team refused to play Montreal because of Robinson, and another called off the game, claiming the electricity had blown out. At a third match, a local police chief,

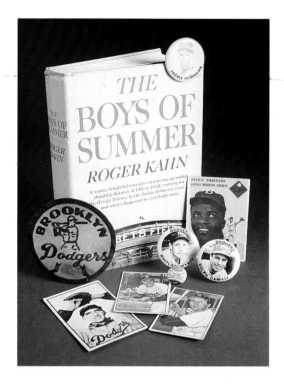

citing Jim Crow laws, stopped the game in the second inning. Of course, Robinson and his wife, Rachel, could not sleep in white hotels; rather, they stayed in black hotels or with black families. Although he was surrounded by bigots in Florida, he persevered.

In his very first minor league game, against the Jersey City Giants, Robinson went four for four with a home run. He continued to play well, but on the road the bigots were always out there, screaming "nigger," throwing black cats, and shoving watermelons toward him. But at

JACKIE ROBINSON

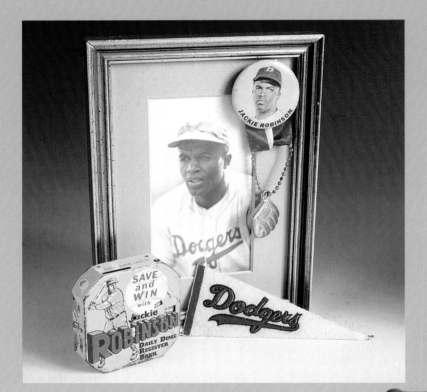

A Jackie Robinson dime savings bank anchors this collage of Robinson collectibles.

Directly below, Robinson autographed this store model bat in 1956.

Bottom, Jackie Robinson's jacket, probably from 1955 or 1956.

What he did, quite simply, was show baseball, and America, that talented blacks were as good as talented whites. Just to do that—to show equality on the field—turned the whole racial thing around. What could blacks do against the best major leaguers was a question argued heatedly for decades. Well, Jackie was the answer. And that answer brought equality in baseball and brought it right away.

—BROADCASTER ART RUST, JR.

You know what he was? He was a run. When he got on base he would steal, get to second on a hit-and-run, stretch a single to a double, go from second to home on a short single. He would score. I saw having Jackie on base as a single run in our favor every time we played. You add a run to all those close games and you see that man was worth 25 to 35 ball games.

—KEN LEHMAN, DODGERS

A kids' Jackie Robinson pencil sharpener.

Robinson was everywhere when he came up: witness *Time* magazine and a dugout full of books.

Dodger lapel wear.

picked a stronger team. In 1946 the Dodgers had almost won another pennant, losing only to the Cardinals, two games to none, in the first-ever playoff for the National League champion. The team was loaded with talent.

The hate was there in the majors as well. Several players on Robinson's own club decided they would circulate a petition in spring training to get him thrown off the Dodgers. But a fuming Leo Durocher met with them at midnight and told them anyone who signed it would be traded the next day; the petition was dropped. Players on other teams also taunted Jackie with racial epithets and insults, including several players on the Cardinals who threatened to strike unless he was removed from baseball. The National League president, Ford Frick, stopped that talk quickly.

The worst race-baiting came from the Philadelphia Phillies, although there were death threats in several cities. The pressure on Robinson was extreme, but decent people came to his aid. After fierce racial shouting at one park, Pee Wee Reese, a Southerner, walked over to a distressed Jackie and put his arm around him, hugging him, to show the bigots in the stands where he stood. In one stadium, opposing players were giving it to Robinson when Eddie Stanky, who had been opposed to

the plate, Robinson was electric, hitting a league-leading .349.

More determined than ever to shatter the color line, that same year Rickey signed two other Negro League stars, Roy Campanella and Don Newcombe, and hid them on a minor league team in Nashua, New Hampshire, where they were subject to little racial abuse. In 1947, wanting to take the heat off Robinson, he moved Dodger spring training to Havana, a city with a large black population. When the season opened, Robinson made history by becoming the first black ever to play on a major league team. He could not have

A late Forties Dodgertown spring training scorecard.

any blacks in the majors back in April, stood in front of their dugout and yelled, "Come out here and yell at someone who doesn't have to take it!"

Several newspaper columnists, notably Walter Winchell and Jimmy Powers, went to bat for Robinson, carrying on a crusade against the Phillies' bigots. National pressure for integration began to build. Then Rickey brought up black pitcher Dan Bankhead, the Cleveland Indians moved up slugger Larry Doby, and the St. Louis Browns signed Willard Brown and Hank Thompson.

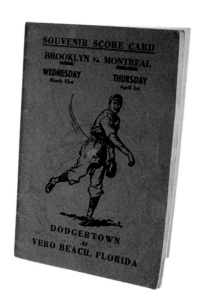

Need some hitting advice? Check out Jackie and Pee Wee on this 45.

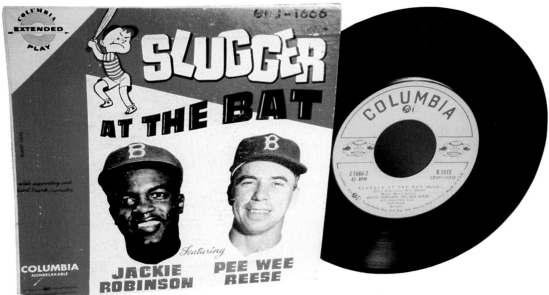

The Topps Company was and still is located in downtown Brooklyn, and although its executives swore they produced the same number of cards for each team, local kids were sure they printed more of the Dodgers. Topps cards of Labine, Jackson, and Walker are shown here with some others.

Soon enough Monte Irvin would go to the Giants and Hank Aaron to the Braves.

Robinson answered critics with his blistering bat. By June, he was averaging .300 and hitting every top pitcher in the league. His fielding was superb, his base stealing astonishing. He was also driving the Dodgers toward a pennant, their first in six years. By the end of 1947 Robinson was named Rookie of the Year by *The Sporting News*. Teams signed a half-dozen other blacks.

Duke Snider saw him as the consummate, well-rounded performer who had an emotional and psychological edge few

possessed. "I suppose people remember him as the man who broke the color line, but I saw Jackie as one of the country's most extraordinary athletes," Snider recalled. "Here was a guy who was All American at football and an even better baseball player. He was superbly skilled and he was smart. He thought his way through a game. And to watch him! What a thrill. When he was on base, every eye in the ballpark was on him, to see him dance off the base or steal. What an exciting player. I think the best way to look at Jackie Robinson is this: when he got to Brooklyn, we won the pennant. Period."

The Duke looks at him that way, but history sees him as "the First." Because of Robinson's skills, personality, and perseverance, the disgraceful color line was shattered and, in just a single season of baseball, the national pastime was integrated forever.

That year and every year afterward, hundreds of organizations tried to heap humanitarian awards on Branch Rickey, the man who integrated baseball. But he refused every one. "There's no point in giving anyone an award for signing a great ballplayer," he shrugged.

Above, Bond Bread jumped on the Robinson bandwagon early, putting Jackie in its 1948 card set.

Left, Dodgers pennants were everywhere in Brooklyn.

CHAPTER FOUR

GLORY DAYS
1947–1955

Following a strong 1946 season in which the Dodgers lost a playoff to the Cards for the pennant, the addition of the electric Jackie Robinson was the final ingredient in the Dodger mix. Thus began the glory years, a ten-year period in which the Dodgers would win the National League pennant six times and finish second three times. Only the Yankees would be more successful during these years.

In addition to the arrival of Robinson and black stars Don Newcombe, Roy Campanella, Junior Gilliam, and Joe Black, the late Forties was a significant time for the Dodgers in other ways too. The end of World War II saw the return of two million GIs to America, and all those Brooklynite vets arrived at Ebbets in droves to see Rickey's hot new 1947 team, anchored by rookie center fielder Duke Snider and first baseman Gil Hodges.

Of all the Dodgers, few had the success and fan appreciation of the Duke and Gil. Snider started slowly in 1947, but by 1949, with help from batting coach George Sisler, he hit his stride with 23 homers and 92 RBIs. For his part the muscular, friendly Snider would become a Brooklyn powerhouse, hitting 316 home runs during the course of his career. He also became part of a raging New York controversy about who was the world's best center fielder—Willie Mays, Mickey Mantle, or the Duke.

No more "Wait Till Next Year" signs at Vero Beach, the training camp of the newly crowned world champs.

71

A Dodger doll, in the middle of this collage, is surrounded by a generation of memorabilia.

Walter Alston was a steady minor league success as manager by 1954 when the Dodgers called him up as skipper. The easygoing Alston won a pennant in two of his first three seasons in Brooklyn and then five more in Los Angeles.

Far right, a Dodger pin.

There was even a song written about the trio. (Incidentally, in the four seasons they all played in New York, Snider smacked the most home runs.) A consistent hitter, at different points in his career the Duke finished among the top three players in home runs, RBIs, average, doubles, triples, hits, and runs.

"We won because we had talent, but we also won because we played for each other, not just for the club," said the Duke. "We genuinely liked each other."

While both were with the Dodgers, from 1947 to 1961, Snider combined with Hodges to hit 745 home runs, the fourth

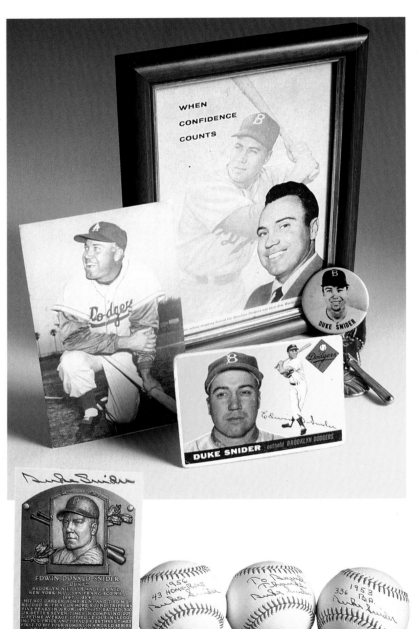

74

highest total in history for two team-mates. Hodges had come up as a strong-armed catcher, but the acquisition of Campanella moved him (happily) to first base. A good pull hitter, he crashed over 100 RBIs seven years in a row and made the All-Star team seven times. He averaged .273 lifetime, and had 370 home runs and 1,274 RBIs. Fans loved him so much that when he was in an 0 for 21 slump against the Yankees in the 1952 World Series, priests and ministers throughout Brooklyn asked parishioners to say a prayer for him. Later, Hodges gained equal fame as a manager when he piloted the "Miracle Mets" of 1969 to their first World Series.

After an extraordinary 1947 season in which the newly dominant Dodgers dazzled the National League, the team moved on to the Series, again against the Yankees. The Bombers made their presence known quickly, taking the first two games at Yankee Stadium. Everyone jumped on the subway for Brooklyn for game three, which the Dodgers won. Then came game four, and another trip

Left and above, who needed kings and queens when Brooklyn had the Duke?

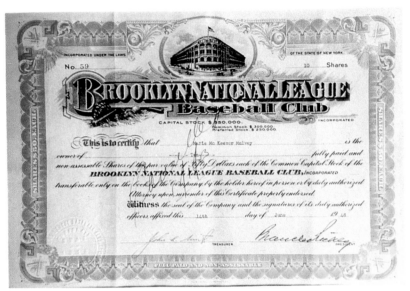

Above, a 1948 certificate for ten shares of the Brooklyn team.

Top right, fifty years on Flatbush was celebrated in this 1948 program.

Below, fans remember the 1949 Series as just another loss to the hated Yankees.

age 23, he was already considered the best and most experienced catcher in baseball.

He would only play ten seasons in the majors, but in those years he became one of the game's great players, winning three MVP awards.

"He was in complete charge of the game," said pitcher Don Newcombe. "He called every pitch perfectly. I only shook him off three times in my career and each time the batter hit a home run on me. He wasn't only good at calling, he would run the whole game. He knew every hitter's slightest move and he'd move all the infielders and outfielders around to fit each hitter. The game was a science to him. He was the best."

Right, burly catcher
Roy Campanella
lives forever in
Cooperstown.

Far right, Campy,
like so many others,
pitched Wheaties.

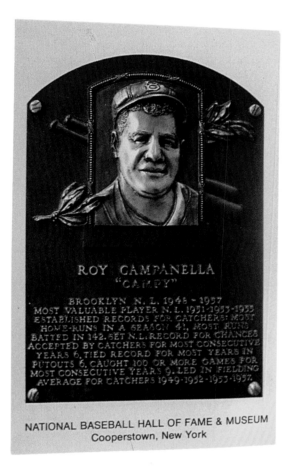

ROY CAMPANELLA
"CAMPY"

BROOKLYN N. L. 1948 ~ 1957
MOST VALUABLE PLAYER N. L. 1951·1953·1955
ESTABLISHED RECORDS FOR CATCHERS: MOST
HOME-RUNS IN A SEASON 41, MOST RUNS
BATTED IN 142·SET N.L.RECORD FOR CHANCES
ACCEPTED BY CATCHERS FOR MOST CONSECUTIVE
YEARS 6, TIED RECORD FOR MOST YEARS IN
PUTOUTS 6· CAUGHT 100 OR MORE GAMES FOR
MOST CONSECUTIVE YEARS 9· LED IN FIELDING
AVERAGE FOR CATCHERS 1949·1952·1953·1957

NATIONAL BASEBALL HALL OF FAME & MUSEUM
Cooperstown, New York

Preacher Roe, another fine Dodger
pitcher, agreed. "He was never wrong.
Never. I threw whatever he told me to
throw."

The Dodgers were a daring team
during those years. The Giants' Sam Jones
once hit Robinson with a pitch, but Jackie
did not charge the mound (he never did).
Instead he simply trotted to first.

"He yelled over to Jones that he was
going to steal second, and he did," remembered Campanella. "Then he told him he'd
steal third, and he did. Jones was completely unnerved by now. Then Jackie
moved off third and told Jones he was
going to steal home—and he did! And we
won that game, 1-0. Now, did Jackie get
even with him or what?"

The Dodgers took the pennant in
1949 and again met the Yankees in the
World Series. And again they lost. The
Yanks took the Series in five games and
Don Newcombe went winless (he would
never win a World Series game). But he
paralyzed the players he did face, and

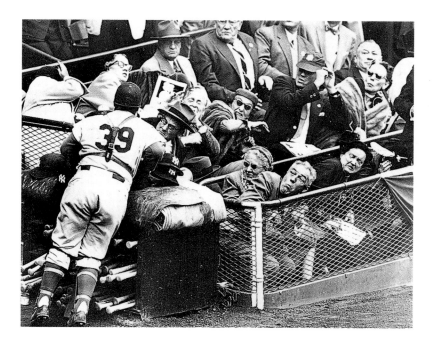

A dramatic World Series catch sends Roy Campanella crashing into the stands.

Pee Wee Reese, captain of the Dodgers, was one of the most admired players of his generation.

years later, despite his stats, Yankees would moan about Big Newk.

"I could never hit Newk. I studied him, analyzed him, thought about him when I went to sleep, but I could never figure him out," admitted Mickey Mantle. "Now, Yogi killed Newk. He used to give me all these tips, but I'd get in there against him in the Series, all of those Series, and he'd handcuff me. Never could touch him. In my 17 years of playing ball, he was the toughest pitcher I ever faced."

The next year the Dodgers were strong and impressive again, but they lost the pennant on the final day of the season to the Philadelphia "Whiz Kids."

Then came the most crushing loss of all, the 1951 pennant. Books have been written about it, poems composed, and disagreements argued long into the night. By mid-August the Dodgers had piled up a seemingly insurmountable 13 1/2-game lead over the Giants with one of the most powerful baseball teams in history. But the Giants shifted into high gear even as the Dodgers began to falter a bit, and at the end of the regular season the two teams were tied. The commissioner then ordered a three-game playoff. The teams split the first two and the Dodgers were leading game three in the ninth inning when relief pitcher Ralph Branca, wearing number 13, served up a home-run ball to

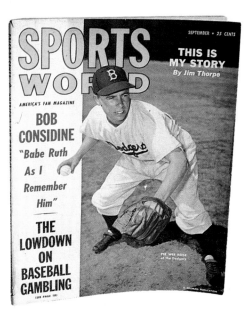

SEPTEMBER · 25 CENTS

SPORTS WORLD

AMERICA'S FAN MAGAZINE

THIS IS MY STORY
By Jim Thorpe

BOB CONSIDINE
"Babe Ruth As I Remember Him"

THE LOWDOWN ON BASEBALL GAMBLING

Showing the form that made him a Hall of Famer, Pee Wee Reese, who just took a toss from Junior Gilliam *(behind him),* **makes the force on the Cubs' Jim Bolger and throws to first.**

Bobby Thomson, the "shot heard round the world" that won the pennant for the Giants.

The Dodgers bounced back in 1952 and 1953, winning back-to-back pennants, but lost the World Series both years to the Yankees. The next season they floundered in second place in the National League when the Giants had one of their best years. Of course second would have been just fine for many teams, but the Dodgers had developed high expectations—so much so that MacPhail, the man responsible for the team's rise almost twenty years before, was quickly fired.

"Those Dodger teams were among the best in the history of the game," insisted the late Yankee pitcher Vic Raschi. "If the Yankees weren't the powerhouse they were, the Dodgers would have been the team taking eight of ten World Series, the team being hailed as the greatest of all time. They just had the bad luck of running into us all the time."

Don Newcombe, their star pitcher, thinks there was more to it than home runs and four-run rallies. Standing in the press box high over Dodger Stadium on a warm summer night, he remembered life as a Dodger.

"We were a team in everything we did. That infield didn't just play baseball every afternoon. Those guys played cards

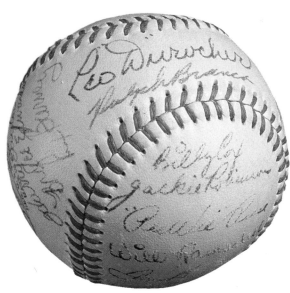

Durocher signed the sweet spot on this ball right next to teammate pitcher Ralph Branca in 1948. Three years later Leo was manager of the Giants when Dodger Branca threw a home-run ball to the Giants' Bobby Thomson in the 1951 playoffs.

with each other every night on the train. We'd eat dinner together, take cabs together, talk in hotel rooms together," recalled Newk, dressed impeccably in a beige-and-white striped suit and carrying a straw hat.

"You'd always have four, five, six guys together. They knew each other's every move, so when a ball was hit between first and second, everybody knew what to do and everybody did it. It was a complete, total team and that's why we won so much," he continued. "And we liked each other. We didn't have feuds on the team. We had feuds with the Giants and the Yankees."

For weeks, people called my house to harass me. They even called my mother and told her to teach her son how to pitch. . . . It's all people talk to me about. I had a full and satisfactory career, but no one talks about that. Now I'm resigned to it. If people haven't forgotten it after 40 years, they never will. I don't mind any more. After all, I know that when I die, the first line in my obituary will be "Ralph Branca, who threw a home run ball to Bobby Thomson, . . ."

—RALPH BRANCA, DODGERS

Duke Snider's 1954 jacket, with signed ball. The Duke became lore as part of the great center-field debate of the Fifties: Who was better, Willie (Mays), Mickey (Mantle), or the Duke?

Right, Don Newcombe, "Big Newk," came to the Dodgers from the Negro Leagues in 1949 and became a star. Lifetime, he posted a 149-90 record, won the Rookie of the Year Award in 1949, MVP and Cy Young Awards in 1956, and was named an All-Star four times.

Below, Don Newcombe, who fashioned a 27-7 record in 1956, holds up the Cy Young and MVP Awards his efforts brought.

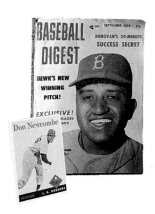

Don Newcombe's jacket.

The Dodgers, like their predecessors from the Forties, Thirties, and Twenties, had fun. Team members were always playing practical jokes or setting up crazy contests. "Once Duke and Zim [Don Zimmer] were daring each other to do things," remembered pitcher Ken Lehman. "It was July of '56. Duke said he could throw a ball over the center-field wall from the front of the dugout and Zim dared him. On just two steps he did it—a 400-foot line drive. Then Zim picked up a ball and he did the same thing. They were laughing their heads off. Then a third guy walked out. I grabbed a ball, too, thinking everybody on the team was going to wing one into the center-field seats, but the third guy was the manager, Walt Alston, and he said the next guy to heave one was going to be fined. So I dropped the ball and Snider and Zimmer walked off, laughing."

Stamp books were sold in the late Forties and early Fifties for every team, but the Dodgers book was the most popular.

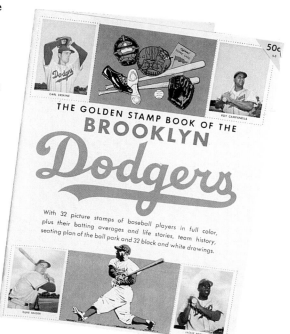

I was traded to the Dodgers and I moved to Brooklyn a few days before my first game. I was walking down a street, in street clothes, on my way to a supermarket a day or two before I joined the team. Two guys stopped me and said, "Hey, you're Elmer Valo. Welcome to Brooklyn!" They knew me from my picture in the paper and they were thrilled, just thrilled, that I was here and playing for their baseball team. I never had a feeling like that in my whole life, not ever.

—ELMER VALO, DODGERS

And life was nice. People loved the Dodgers. From Coney Island and Canarsie to Flatbush and Red Hook to the subway station underneath Borough Hall, they were the neighborhood's team. They even had their own rollicking fight song, "Follow the Dodgers."

The 1950s saw Dodgers souvenir sales flood Ebbets and spill over onto Bedford Avenue. There had always been Dodgers memorabilia, even back to the turn of the century, but during the Fifties manufacturers, and the team itself, produced a deluge of material. New printing technology available by 1950 enabled the major league teams to produce inexpensive, glossy paper programs and yearbooks, which were easy to roll up, stuff in your pocket for the subway ride, and then unroll at home. Dodgers pennants, buttons, hats, and dolls were also mass marketed (Jackie Robinson had his very own personal mass-produced doll). Comics, players photos, and books on the team were also snapped up by eager fans.

"Playing for the Dodgers in the Fifties was like playing for some small 3,000-person town in the Thirties. It was this huge place, Brooklyn, yet everybody knew everybody. My friends weren't just the ballplayers, they were the people who lived on my block, the guy who ran the candy store, everybody," said Duke Snider.

What little kid wouldn't want his very own Jackie Robinson doll? The flood of Jackie souvenirs provided a strong indication of the success of baseball's integration. Blacks, banned from baseball for so long, suddenly became heroes.

The Dodgers always had time for the fans, especially the kids in the neighborhood. One of the friendliest was Campanella, arguably the best catcher the game has ever seen.

"I lived a few houses down from Campy when I was a kid," said Elwin Rawlins, now a lawyer in Wisconsin. "After a game, we'd wait outside his stoop till he came home and we'd talk to him. He'd joke with us, kid around, sign lots of

By the early Fifties there were Jackie bronzes, pennants, bats, and pictures. More than any other development, Robinson's arrival was responsible for a dramatic increase in the creation of Dodger souvenirs.

The 1955 Dodgers, an all-star roster including Koufax, Campanella, Hodges, Newcombe, Snider, and Robinson.

The Dodgers instructed kids on how to play the game on this record.

autographs, tell us stories—win or lose. I never saw Campy mad or depressed, never. And he loved us kids, just loved us."

In 1955 it finally happened: the Dodgers finally captured the Holy Grail, the World Series, although in true Dodger fashion they went about it all wrong. The team had an inexperienced manager, Walter Alston, known for his hunches and not his experience, and their opponent, as always, was the crosstown Yankees. Managed by the Ol' Perfessor, Casey Stengel, the

Rival 1953 World Series managers Chuck Dressen and Casey Stengel poke their heads through a floral wreath during the Dodgers-Yankees face-off.

A championship banner from 1955.

Bronx Bombers had tremendous hitting with Mantle, Berra, and others, and fantastic pitching led by Whitey Ford, but they had barely won the pennant in the American League. In the first two games of the Series, at Yankee Stadium, the Yanks sneaked by the Dodgers 6-5 and 4-2. As the Dodgers, the Yankees, the press, and the good residents of Flatbush Avenue knew, no team down two games to none had ever come back to win the World Series, and the prospects seemed less likely against the powerhouse Yankees.

After all these years, though, the Dodgers were not about to die. They beat the Yanks in games three and four at Ebbets amid the roars and howls of their faithful. For game five, Alston went with a gut instinct and yanked the scheduled Newcombe, who never did well in the October Classic, in favor of rookie Roger Craig, who came through for the win. Then the Yankees took game six and it all came down to a final match at Yankee Stadium with the Dodgers' Johnny Podres facing Tommy Byrne, who had posted a sensational 16-5 mark that year. The Bums built a rocky 2-0 lead going into the seventh and Brooklyn fans, disappointed so often, waited for doomsday. With two men on in the bottom of the seventh, it seemed to come. Yogi Berra hit a sure triple down the line toward the left-field

Twenty-three-year-old rookie Johnny Podres's face scrunches up as he delivers the final pitch of the 1955 World Series, the Dodgers' first world championship.

corner. But in one of the great plays in Series history, left fielder Sandy Amoros came from out of nowhere and speared the ball, then turned and doubled Gil McDougald off first to end the inning.

"Did I think he'd catch that ball?" asked McDougald years later. "I didn't think anybody could catch that ball. Whenever I see that video I still think that ball is going to drop."

Podres, breathing a huge sigh of relief, held firm against the vaunted Yankee bats and they threatened no more. The game ended on a routine ground out and with that the Dodgers won their first World Series, beating the invincible Yankees, the crosstown Yankees, the cor-

Three front-page views of Sandy Amoros's miraculous catch of Yogi Berra's drive in the last game of the 1955 Series.

porate Yankees. The blue collar boys from Flatbush had finally beaten the penthouse crowd from Manhattan.

In the Dodgers locker room, there was quiet. "We were shocked. We weren't slapping each other on the back or anything like that. We just kind of savored it. We had worked very hard for it, for years, and we finally did it. That was a nice feeling," said Carl Erskine, a.k.a. "Oisk," who pitched in game four.

The players may have been quiet, but outside, in the real world, from Bensonhurst to Canarsie, from Coney Island to Prospect Park, all of Brooklyn celebrated. The hard-luck Dodgers were gone. They were Bums no more.

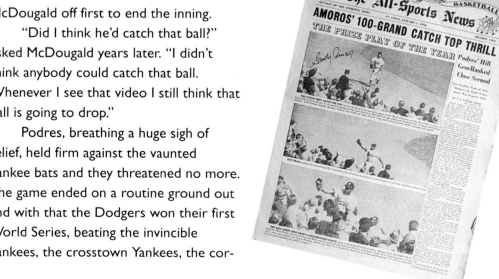

CHAPTER FIVE

CALIFORNIA, HERE WE COME

1956–1963

The noise at Ebbets Field shook the red-brick exterior of the old bandbox ballpark in the summer of 1956. The world champion Dodgers, loaded with an All-Star lineup and a deadly pitching staff, mowed down the National League again and won another pennant, only to lose in the World Series to the Yankees.

There was no noise out at Chavez Ravine, the enormous, hilly, windswept meadow that sat in the heart of Los Angeles overlooking the skyscrapers of the business district. A soft breeze blew the high, unkempt grass, and the palm trees stretched toward the sky.

A year later, unable to get officials in New York to help him build a new stadium in Brooklyn, Dodgers owner Walter O'Malley announced that he was leaving Brooklyn and taking the Dodgers to L.A., where he would build baseball's loveliest stadium at Chavez Ravine. He couldn't stay in Brooklyn, he declared, because Ebbets was too old and too small. Plus there was no parking. Plus the residents of New York were moving to Long Island, he decided. Convinced that he had no future in Brooklyn, O'Malley secretly negotiated to move west with Los Angeles mayor Norris Poulson during the course of 1956 and 1957. Giants' owner Horace Stoneham, whose team's attendance had shrunk in the years following their 1954 world championship, was negotiating at the same time

Players join L.A. officials in holding up a huge World Championship flag.

Above, Walter O'Malley with New York mayor Robert Wagner and Giants' owner Horace Stoneham (*left to right*) at a press conference concerning the city's efforts to keep the Dodgers and the Giants.

Upper right, a Dodgers sun cap.

Right, a Dodgers pin.

to transplant his team to San Francisco.

To Dodgers fans in Brooklyn, where the team had played for 67 years, the move was unthinkable. They were crushed. "I loved the Dodgers completely. I was in shock for years after they left Brooklyn," averred longtime fan Ernie Hahl, who now lives in Parsippany, New Jersey. "They just abandoned us. It was cold, cruel, and heartless. They couldn't make enough money in Brooklyn, so they went to Los Angeles. I stopped rooting for them the minute their plane to L.A. took off. I never talked about them again or read about them in the newspapers. They weren't my team anymore. They were someone else's team. Let someone else root for them, I wouldn't."

The fans had tried hard to keep their Dodgers in the neighborhood. Thousands of them wrote letters to Mayor Robert Wagner urging him to do whatever he could to keep the Dodgers home. Thousands more wrote to the local newspapers. Everyone failed.

The Dodgers' move was a stunner for several reasons. Sure, other teams had moved—the Boston Braves had left for Milwaukee, half way across America, just five years before. But the Braves were a lowly baseball team, while the Dodgers were world champs in 1955 and pennant winners in 1956. The Dodgers also took

Dodgers World
Series tickets.

The Dodger fans in L.A. were, right away, different from the fans in Brooklyn. Today, they are very different from the old Brooklyn fans. They are more laid back. . . . To compare L.A. fans to Brooklyn fans isn't fair because back in the Fifties no other team had fans like the people in Brooklyn. You'll just never have that closeness between team and fans again in America. Never.

—DON DRYSDALE, DODGERS

the Giants with them, leaving fans with no National League team. Indeed the only team left in the whole city was the Yankees, the American League Yankees, the hated Yankees—and no loyal Dodger fan would EVER switch and cheer for the Yankees. The Dodgers' move crushed Brooklynites and left a hole in the heart of the borough as wide as the Brooklyn Bridge.

While Brooklynites mourned bitterly, the Dodgers moved easily into the welcoming arms of their adoptive home. Los Angeles had never had a major league baseball team before, but its citizens were enthusiastic fans. When O'Malley decided to trade the streetlights of Flatbush for the bending palm trees of Los Angeles, he wasn't exactly bringing the area its first taste of professional baseball. Minor league teams had played in balmy Los Angeles since the turn of the century. L.A. was a baseball-rich area, and it was that love affair with the minor league teams that built the foundation for the Dodgers.

The first minor league team in Los Angeles had competed in the California League in the summer of 1893, even playing a night game against Stockton with kerosene lamps rigged to four tall poles. The center fielder on the team had been none other than the flamboyant Billy Sunday, who went on to become a famous

Above, these 1950s Topps cards captured the joy of the Dodgers in those years.

Below, is this power or what? From top to bottom, the game-used bats of Roy Campanella (242 home runs in the major leagues, over 200 in the Negro Leagues),

Duke Snider (407 home runs), Gil Hodges (370 home runs), Zack Wheat (.317 lifetime average), and Jackie Robinson (.311 lifetime).

evangelist. Then in 1903 Los Angeles landed a team in the historic Pacific Coast League; it played its games at Chutes Park until 1911 and then moved over to Washington Park.

Baseball became so popular that a second Pacific Coast League team came to town in 1909 and played its game in suburban Vernon. The Vernon franchise was shifted to San Francisco in 1925, the same year that a Utah team was moved to Vernon by owner William Wrigley, Jr., also owner of the Chicago Cubs. Wrigley named his team, appropriately, the Hollywood Stars, and built a 22,000-seat, $1.1 million park called Wrigley Field, which hosted a night game three years before the majors. The L.A. team and the Stars consistently drew 10,000 to 20,000 fans per game, leading city officials constantly to press for a major league franchise.

Twice they almost got one. In 1942 Don Barnes, owner of the St. Louis Browns, said he would jump to Los Angeles, but World War II ended his plans. In 1953 the Browns once again decided to move west, but L.A. Coliseum officials said they would not convert for baseball and the deal died.

The Dodgers finally arrived after O'Malley convinced Coliseum officials that the stadium could be converted at a cost of only $200,000. The problem with the

Coliseum, though, was that it was a football stadium (it had been home to the 1932 Olympics as well). The Dodgers never intended to stay there long, but in the interim a baseball field was carefully shoehorned in. The results were awful. To make it fit, the sidewall of seats on the side that would serve as the left-field wall was only 251 feet from home plate, a long spit of chewing tobacco. Conversely, right field extended out into the football field and the right field wall was positioned way out at 440 feet, the farthest in all of baseball. Fans sitting behind the wall were another good 30 yards back in the football seats. To make certain Babe Ruth's home-run record wasn't broken in one week by batters knocking balls over the short porch in left, the Coliseum also put up a "Chinese screen," which rose 40 feet.

Despite problems with the park, over 78,000 people turned out for the Dodgers' first home game at the Coliseum and more would follow. The team would set dozens of attendance records in the Coliseum. City fathers were thrilled. "The Dodgers make Los Angeles a big league city in every way," declared Mayor Poulson.

For its part, the team fell apart. After finishing third in Brooklyn in 1957, they crashed to a miserable seventh in sunny Los Angeles in 1958. Many factors

were at work. That winter, Roy Campanella had been paralyzed for life in a tragic automobile accident. (A tribute to Campy would draw 93,000 fans.) Pee Wee Reese was getting old. Newcombe, who had been the Cy Young Award winner in 1956, had fallen onto hard times as a pitcher and was traded in the middle of the 1958 season. The rest of the pitching staff was mediocre, with Don Drysdale going 12-13, Podres 13-15, and Sandy Koufax 11-11.

Broadcasters Vin Scully and Jerry Doggett were featured in this issue of "Meet the Dodger Family." Perhaps more than anything, the lyrical radio voice of Scully in the soft California night, carefully explaining major league baseball, helped establish the Dodgers quickly in California.

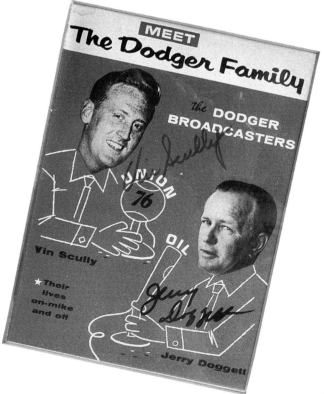

I nearly cried when I heard the Brooklyn Dodgers were moving here. I went to their very first game, in the Coliseum, where they had that crazy fence in left field. I went to Campy's tribute and lit a candle. I loved every game and every season and every player.

—JACK ZITTRER, FAN, SHERMAN OAKS, CALIFORNIA

I was a Dodger fan in 1955 when they won the World Series back in Brooklyn. I never, ever thought they'd move here. The arrival of the Dodgers was, to me at ten, the greatest event in history.

—DAN RICE, FAN, PALMDALE, CALIFORNIA

The Dodgers became the first team in baseball to buy their own plane, the Kay O II.

Duke Snider hit 407 home runs in his career, including one that shattered a clock on a wall above the centerfield seats in Saint Louis.

Gil Hodges's Gold Glove Award from 1957.

To make matters worse, the Dodgers battled a coast-to-coast schedule. "When we played in Brooklyn our farthest game was in St. Louis," said Joe Pignatano, a Dodgers catcher in Brooklyn in 1957 and L.A. in 1958. "Road trips lasted just two weeks. In California, 3,000 miles from home, we flew everywhere. There were no teams nearby, so every game was a long flight. Our road trips would last 28, 30 days. That meant all those planes and all those hotels and all that time away from home. It really wore you out. We spent that whole first year just trying to adjust. It was tough."

And Los Angeles was definitely not Brooklyn. It took some orientation. "I'd always leave my house an hour ahead of time because I'd always get lost driving on those freeways," said Dodger second baseman Charlie Neal, hero of the '59 Series. "I'd never take the right exit and go through half of California just to make a U turn. They should have given us highway maps as well as lockers."

"It was a combination of things," added Drysdale. "We had trouble getting used to the screen and a new field. Power lefties had trouble with that deep right field fence. The travel hurt. People couldn't adjust. We were just a mess," he said. "But after one year, we bounced right back."

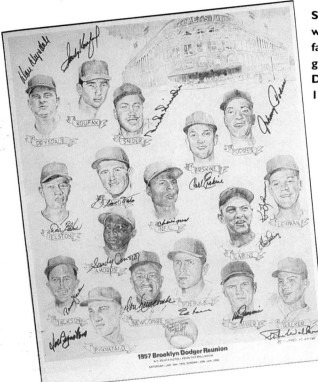

Somehow, some way, L.A. Dodgers fan Rafael Sanchez got all of these Dodgers to sign this 1957 reunion poster.

1957 Brooklyn Dodger Reunion

When we first moved to L.A. the traveling was terrible. I remember on one road trip we were gone three weeks. My daughter was born back in L.A. and I kept up with her progress by seeing pictures of her in the newspapers in each different city we played. When you travel that much, you just get worn out. You're constantly flying across time zones, moving in and out of ballparks and hotels. It's tough.

—DON DRYSDALE, DODGERS

They certainly did. In 1959 veteran Don Zimmer replaced a retired Reese. Speedster Maury Wills was acquired. Wally Moon, who would spend all season smashing line drives off the screen, came over from the Cardinals. Big Frank Howard, all 6'6" of him, was brought up from the minors. Sandy Koufax matured as a pitcher and in midseason fanned 16 Phillies in one game. "We had a great team, and we needed it in the division we were in," said Wills.

The Dodgers were in a race with the Giants and Braves for the crown right to the last day of the season, which ended with the Dodgers and Braves tied. In a playoff series, the Dodgers won the pennant and the right to meet the Chicago White Sox in the World Series.

The Dodgers arrived in Chicago dead tired, just a day after finishing the playoffs with the Braves. They were pounded in game one, 11-0, and it looked like a debacle. But they rallied and took game two, 4-3, before returning to the Coliseum, where 92,000 turned out to see them win game three. Gil Hodges won game four with a home run. The Dodgers won the Series four games to two, the first world championship for any West Coast team.

The 1959 World Series win accomplished several important things for the

Top, the *Los Angeles Mirror News* isn't around any more, but the Dodgers are. This was opening-day issue for the Coliseum in 1958.

Dodgers. Most immediately it showed that 1958 was a transition year, nothing more, and that the Dodgers had the same strong club on the West Coast that they had had back East. The win ended the decade on a high note for the Dodgers, but it also established them as L.A.'s team—they weren't the Brooklyn Dodgers anymore, and they never would be. People in Los Angeles talked only of the 1959 world champions; they had no knowledge of the angst created by the Yankees all of those years. The L.A. fans drove to the ballpark on complicated freeway routes. They didn't dodge trolleys to get there and they didn't ride subways. The Californians were as laid-back as Brooklynites were aggressive. Some fans even brought small barbecue spits to the Coliseum and cooked hamburgers and hot dogs while they watched the game. Everything was different now. They didn't remember

The local press caught the fever big in 1959.

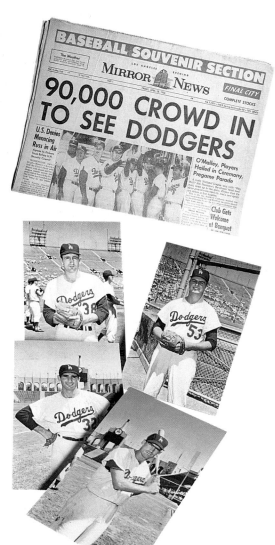

These picture cards were issued by the Dodgers in 1958 when they moved to the Coliseum, featuring (*clockwise from lower left*)

Sandy Koufax, Roger Craig, Don Drysdale, and Wally Moon, whose "Moon Shots" peppered the makeshift wall in left field.

97

Right, field credentials, a ticket stub, and a program from the 1959 World Series, which really established the Dodgers as West Coast icons and whitewashed their image as Bums.

Above, Wally Moon scores in the second inning of game four in the 1959 World Series, the Dodgers' first in California.

Right, programs from the first three games at the Coliseum in the 1959 October Classic.

Uncle Robbie, or Boom-Boom Beck, or Charlie Ebbets, and they didn't care. And they didn't call their team "the Bums." The Dodgers were the Los Angeles team now, once and forever. An era had definitely ended and another had begun.

Following the 1959 world championship, the Dodgers slipped somewhat. They ended up fourth in 1960, thirteen games out, but climbed back to second, just four out, in 1961. Their rivalry with the Giants continued, although now the two teams had to fly up and down the coast rather than ride across town to meet each other. Increasingly the Dodgers also became part of the daily life of the City of Angels. Manager Alston and many of the players were regular after-dinner speakers, Walter O'Malley had become a figure in the community, and a television show was created called "Meet the Dodgers," featuring an interview with a different player each week. Someone even wrote a song entitled "We Love the Dodgers," which was just as popular as the old "Follow the Dodgers" was back in Brooklyn. More and more movie stars started coming to games as the Dodgers won. Team members would look up into the stands and spot the stars of films they had seen that weekend. "Everywhere you

I think I was nine or ten when I came to Dodger Stadium for the first time. Walter O'Malley had a Boy Scout Day each year. If you came to the game in your Boy Scout uniform, you got in free. So I went with the others in my troop. I went once a summer each year I was a Boy Scout and then I just fell in love with the team.

— CHEZ, FAN, LOS ANGELES

Above left, th ernous Colis spotlightec 1959 char flag.

Abov An fe

99

This 1958 photo of the Los Angeles Coliseum from a high row shows how large crowds were and how the ballfield was sandwiched into the old football stadium, which was also home of the 1932 Olympics.

Don Drysdale and others signed this ball.

looked there were movie stars," said Charlie Neal. "A simple night game was like the Oscars."

Third baseman Ransom Jackson remembered showing up at the stadium at the start of the 1962 season: "I came to the stadium and this guy walks over to my car and says he's on this fans committee to help ballplayers orient themselves to the new stadium. He said he'd show me around, and he did, giving me a complete tour of the stadium. It was Danny Kaye!"

The Dodgers got a lift by opening 1962 in brand-new Dodger Stadium. They had never intended to stay in the terrible Coliseum for long, and now it was gone, replaced by a paradisiacal new stadium

surrounded by lawns, gardens, and palm trees. This would be the setting for yet another incredible pennant race with the Giants, one as ferocious and exciting as the barnburner of 1951.

On the bench that year were stars like Junior Gilliam, Ron Fairly, Johnny Roseboro, Daryl Spencer, and Willie Davis. But 1962 was Don Drysdale's year. Don was a big handsome man, and out in Hollywood he landed a dozen bit parts in television shows on his name and looks. But he was also a workhorse, leading the league in starts several years. He was a good hitter, too, batting .300 one season, but what he did best was win. The sidearmer won 25 in 1962, 209 lifetime, and set the consecutive scoreless innings

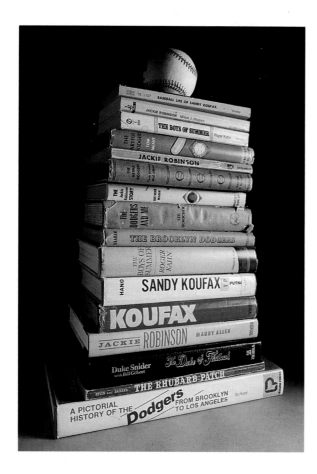

He was such a powerful pitcher in 1962 that he had won 14 by the All-Star break and he and Koufax had propelled Los Angeles into first place. Then, on July 17, Koufax suffered an injury that kayoed him for much of the season. He had been as hot as Drysdale up to that point with 13 wins, and his loss hurt dearly, particularly at the end of the season when the Dodgers slumped badly. While they were on a losing streak, dropping 10 of 13 games, the Giants, led by Willie Mays, Orlando Cepeda, and Willie McCovey, were staging yet another Cinderella comeback, winning game after game and pulling closer and closer to the first-place Dodgers. Finally on the last day of the season the Giants won, the Dodgers lost, and the two teams ended up tied for first. Just as they did back in 1951, the Dodgers lost a three-game playoff and missed the World Series with perhaps the strongest team since the Boys of Summer squads back in Brooklyn in the Fifties.

Baseball 101, Dodgers' style: a coffee table book on the Dodgers holds up a Tower of Babel worth of works on the Dodgers, from Red Barber's 1949 classic, *The Rhubarb Patch,* to several biographies of Sandy Koufax.

record with 58²/₃ in 1968. With Koufax, he helped the Dodgers finish first four out of five years in the mid-Sixties.

Drysdale was notorious for hitting batters—he beaned 154 lifetime, a record. His philosophy was simple: "You hit one of my guys, I hit two of yours. You hit two of mine, I deck four of yours. Simple math, really, pretty easy to understand," he remarked. "They understood."

If the 1962 Dodger team was great, the 1963 squad was even better. Changes were made that strengthened the team, although some were not popular with fans. Aging Duke Snider was traded to the Mets, Don Zimmer and Ed Roebuck were traded, and so was Daryl Spencer. A very

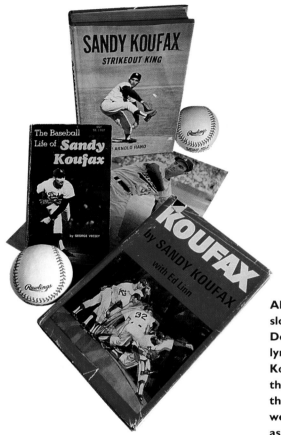

Although he started slowly for the Dodgers in Brooklyn, by 1963 Sandy Koufax had become the best pitcher in the game. L. A. fans were wild over him, as you can see from the plethora of books and magazine stories.

Sandy Koufax worked hard. People forget he started out in Brooklyn with a couple of so-so seasons. He worked hard, found his delivery, and became the best pitcher in baseball. When he was on, nobody, I mean nobody, could touch him.

—Joe Pignatano, Dodgers

unhappy Moose Skowron was acquired from the Yankees. There was bigger news than that, though, news that would make the Dodger blue the brightest ever—Sandy Koufax, probably the best pitcher in baseball (and if it wasn't him it was Drysdale), was healthy.

Koufax hadn't always been regarded so highly. A thin, muscular pitcher with tremendously strong arms, he had exhibited lackluster pitching in both Brooklyn and L.A., and as late as 1960 he was having losing seasons. In 1961 the good-looking pitcher with the curly black hair finally gained the control he needed; posting an 18-13 season, he was on his way. He won 14 in 1962 before his injury, and the next season he bloomed further, winning 25. Koufax's transformation was no fluke—he won 19 the next year, 26 in 1965, and 27 in 1966.

Lifetime, Sandy's record was 165-87, but his pride and joy were four no-hitters, one of them a perfect game. With soft eyes that turned into lasers when he stared down a batter and a motion that carefully concealed the ball until the very last millisecond, he produced a blazing fastball that few could touch. He fanned 269 in 1961 and then turned it up a notch, fanning more and more until he struck out 382 in 1965. "Whenever we had a tight situation, I'd go to the mound and ask him

An enthusiastic Dodgers memorabilia collector has dozens of press and commemorative pins, including these two. The top commemorates the 1959 World Series in the Coliseum, the bottom, the 1963 World Series at Dodger Stadium.

what he wanted to do. The answer was always the same: 'heat,'" said catcher Johnny Roseboro.

Koufax had such control that his ERA in his final year was 1.73. He won three Cy Young Awards and an MVP award and his great seasons led the Dodgers to three pennants; 1963 would be his greatest.

After an impressive spring training in which Koufax took to the mound and fanned 13 Chicago White Sox, the Dodgers looked very ready to take the National League pennant and the world championship they should have had the year before. But once the season started they couldn't do anything right. Hitters struggled at the plate and the pitchers struggled on the mound. In May they were in sixth place and not moving. Then, on May 11, Koufax tossed a no-hitter against the hated Giants, his second, and that one evening turned the Dodgers around. Slowly, ever so slowly, Los Angeles started to climb the standings. By late June, they were neck and neck with both the Giants and Cardinals and by early July they were in first, barely.

The Giants remained hot and the Cards got even hotter. Riding the sizzling arms of Drysdale and Koufax, they stayed in first and late in the season swept a series with the Cardinals after the Cards

had won 19 of 20 games. That did it. The pennant was theirs.

A key was the pitching of Drysdale. That season he led the league in games started and innings pitched, as he had the previous year and would do the following season. He was such a workhorse that he managed to lose 17 games and still have a winning season (he won 19). A few breaks here and there and he could have won more than Koufax. Everyone marveled at Koufax's 306 strikeouts but Drysdale fanned 251. Every day that he took the mound he was part of the lethal L.A. pitching tandem. Batters got no rest in southern California that summer.

Tommy Davis's hitting, some of the best in Dodger history, also fueled the

Hard-hitting Tommy Davis is one of the most under-appreciated of the Dodgers. Although he played in the shadows of Koufax and Drysdale and had to compete with the records established by Snider, he carved out an amazing career in L.A., winning two batting crowns in 1962 and 1963. Davis also had won the batting crown in the Midwest League in 1960 and the Pacific Coast League in 1961, making him the only man to win consecutive titles in three different professional leagues four years in a row.

Maybe the best souvenir of all: a program from the 1963 four-game destruction of the hated Yankees.

team that year. His sizzling bat had attracted Alston from the depths of the Dodgers' well stocked minor league pond, where Davis had won batting titles in not one but two different leagues. He was just as good in the majors, winning back-to-back batting crowns in 1962 and 1963 (the first to achieve that feat since Stan Musial a decade earlier) and hitting .400 in the 1963 World Series.

Despite Davis's heroics, the 1963 World Series would not be easy. The Dodgers had experienced a fine year, with Drysdale and Koufax winning 44 games between them. Frank Howard hit 28 homers and Tommy Davis averaged .326. But in October they met their nemesis from the old neighborhood, the Yankees. This was one of the best Yankee teams ever, even with an injured Mickey Mantle who only played in 65 games. The Bronx Bombers' pitching staff was as sturdy as ever—Whitey Ford won 24, Jim Bouton 21, and Ralph Terry 17. At the plate, the Yankees had four sluggers who hit over 20 homers—Roger Maris, Joe Pepitone, Tom Tresh, and Elston Howard. And in Bobby Richardson, Clete Boyer, and Tony Kubek they had one of the best infields in baseball. The Yankees overpowered the American League that year, winning 104 games and taking the pennant by a runaway 10 1/2 games. For the heavy favorites,

Fellow Dodgers mob pitcher Sandy Koufax after winning game one of the 1963 World Series. Koufax recorded 15 strikeouts, a single-game Series record.

1963
WORLD SERIES
DODGER STADIUM
LOS ANGELES, CALIFORNIA

WORKING PRESS,
RADIO TELEVISION
AND
PHOTOGRAPHER

DAVID DYER

LOS ANGELES ANGELS

AISLE 3 ROW K SEAT 17

GREEN LEVEL — PRESS BOX

ENTER AT
WORLD SERIES PRESS GATE
THROUGH LOT 4 (Green Level)

SUBJECT TO CONDITIONS
ON BACK
Los Angeles Dodgers Inc., Agent

GOOD FOR ADMISSION AT
PRESS GATE ON GAME

4 5 X

A press credential from the 1963 World Series.

the World Series would not be a problem.

Nobody told that to the Dodgers, however. All they knew was that in the seven previous World Series against the Yankees, they had lost six. There was some accounting for past sins to be done.

Yankee Stadium was jammed for the first game as 67,000 New Yorkers (including many old Brooklyn Dodgers fans) lay in wait for a blowout. They got one, too, but it was a Dodger blowout. Koufax

faced Whitey Ford, who spent the afternoon as an interested spectator. Koufax mowed down the fearsome Yankee batting order, setting a World Series record as he struck out 15. And to pour salt into pinstripe wounds, who would knock in two runs to lead Los Angeles to a 5-2 victory but old Moose Skowron, whom the Yankees had traded to the Dodgers.

Game two was no better for the team that won 104 games. Alston threw

105

Johnny Podres at them this time, the same Johnny Podres who had beat them as a kid to win the Series back in 1955. A grizzled veteran now, Podres trumped them again, 4-1, and who should hit a Dodger home run but good old Moose Skowron.

Game three was Big D's turn. Drysdale proved very quickly why he had won the Cy Young Award the summer before, by throwing a three-hit shutout. The Dodgers only got one run themselves but it was all they needed.

It was inconceivable that any team could sweep the Yankees—it had never been done, it just couldn't happen—but at 0-3, that's just what it looked like. The

Dodgers put the best pitcher in the National League, Koufax, on the mound for game four and the Yanks put up the best pitcher in the American League, Ford. It was going to be a pitchers' duel and a pitchers' dream.

Frank Howard hit a home run for the Dodgers and a hobbled Mantle socked one for the Yanks, but that was just about all the firepower either team produced as Koufax and Ford wove their magic. Then somehow Yankee first baseman Joe Pepitone lost a routine throw from third. Jim Gilliam raced from first to third on the error and scored on a sacrifice fly. Koufax held and the Dodgers won the Series, 4-0, absolutely humiliating one of the best Yankee teams of all time.

It was a World Series that had ramifications throughout baseball for decades. Over in the American League, it set the stage for the demise of the Yankees. The Series sweep on the field meant a sweep in the front office, too, and by 1965 the Yanks would tumble to a lowly sixth place, ceasing to present a real threat in the American League for more than a decade. But the Dodgers' star was on the rise. Along with the 1959 championship, the 1963 triumph firmly established them as the powerhouse of the National League and certainly solidified Walt Alston as the team's manager. The Series also estab-

Program from 1963 Series at Dodger Stadium, signed by Sandy Koufax, Don Drysdale, Ron Fairly, and Maury Wills.

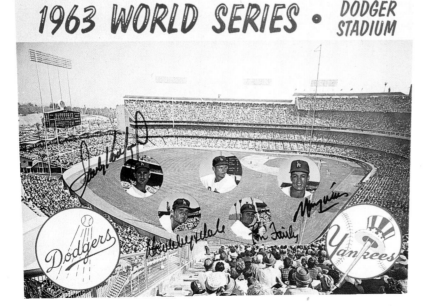

lished the legend of Koufax and Drysdale as a lethal combination. The Dodgers, a team that had become great in the late Forties and Fifties in Brooklyn, had done it again in California, becoming a bicoastal dynasty.

Left, at exactly 10:15 P.M., on May 11, 1964, Sandy Koufax threw the final pitch of his second no-hitter, beating the Giants 8-0. Sandy tossed four no-hitters in his career, the last one a perfect game.

Above, commemorative mugs from the 1959 and 1963 world championships.

Each player is mentioned on this nice 1963 championship pennant.

THE DYNAMIC DUO & OTHER STARS

1964–1979

After an almost-pennant in 1962 and the destruction of the Yankees in 1963, fans might have expected the Dodgers to win at least 140 games the next year. Well, as happens so often in sports, the Dodgers slumped badly. If they were public officials, they would have been run out of town.

The awful lore of '64 started right away, in spring training, when the world champs won nine and lost 16. Frank Howard reported overweight and Koufax complained that his $70,000 salary was not enough. After the season started, Johnny Podres got hit by a pitch that chipped a bone, and he was lost for the year. The team did not have a single .300 hitter or anyone with 100 RBIs. By the All-Star break the Dodgers were stalled in fifth place and never did much better, finishing the year in sixth. Their 80-82 record was their first losing year since 1958. The only highlight was Koufax's third no-hitter.

The front office was furious and General Manager Buzzy Bavasi did more trading than the captains of Chinese junks in Hong Kong Harbor. The first thing he did was get rid of nearly the entire coaching staff (Alston, of course, was there forever). Bavasi ditched Leo Durocher, Pete Reiser, Joe Becker, and Greg Mulleavy, and brought in Junior Gilliam, Danny Ozark, Preston Gomez, and Lefty Phillips. Among players, the

Sandy Koufax celebrates his fourth no-hitter with four "0" baseballs. Only Nolan Ryan tossed more.

A pin from spring training at Dodgertown, early Sixties.

first big head to roll was that of Frank Howard, who had hit 24 homers in 1964. He was traded along with Ken McMullen and pitchers Phil Ortega and Pete Richert. First baseman Ron Fairly was shoved into the outfield to make room for Wes Parker, and a rookie named Jim Lefebvre was installed at second base. Koufax, who arrived at spring training with a swollen arm, was put right back on his plane and told to get well and get well quick. Management let it be known that more blood would flow, and quickly, if the Dodgers didn't do well right away.

People listened. Drysdale won the opener against the Mets on a four-hitter. A few days later in his first start, Koufax beat the Phillies on a five-hitter. Tommy Davis then broke an ankle and was out three

months, but sub Lou Johnson filled in well, hitting .259 with 12 home runs. The Dodgers had a tough race in front of them, though, with the Braves, Reds, and Giants all challenging them for the pennant.

Los Angeles moved into first place briefly in July, then stumbled. It was a heated and sometimes ugly race. Hank Aaron went public and called Drysdale a spitball pitcher. Giants mound ace Juan Marichal, enraged that Dodger catcher Roseboro threw a ball back to the pitcher close to his head, hit him over the head with his bat, starting a violent melee. By early September the Dodgers had faded and were down 4½ games.

The dynamic duo, Koufax and Drysdale, came to the rescue. Koufax hurled his fourth no-hitter, a perfect game, on September 9, and Drysdale won his twentieth game on September 17 (Koufax went on to win 26). The two sparked the team to a 13-game winning streak that carried them into first place and the pennant, a slender two games ahead of the Giants.

The Dodgers met the Minnesota Twins in the World Series. The Twins had fine pitching in Mudcat Grant and Jim Kaat, but they had even better strength in their batting order with Tony Oliva (.321), Jimmie Hall (.285), and Harmon Killebrew (25 home runs). As the Series began the

Twins jumped out to a two-game lead at home, but Dodger pitcher Claude Osteen shut them down in Los Angeles on a five-hitter. Drysdale won game four on another five-hitter, followed by Koufax's four-hitter in game five. The Series went back to Minnesota and the Twins' Grant won game six, 5-1, setting the stage for a dramatic final-game confrontation.

The match was a quiet drama. Lou Johnson, a substitute who had wound up playing most of the year, hit a home run to put L.A. ahead, and Wes Parker drove in Ron Fairly for a second run. That's all the team needed because Koufax, pitching on just two days' rest, tossed a three-hit shutout. The Dodgers had won their third world championship in seven years.

Above, the Dodgers took on the Twins in 1965 and were heavy favorites, but the Twins beat Koufax and Drysdale in the first two games. Sandy came back in the final game to hurl a winning shutout.

Right, fans could mount pins on this L.A. ballfield plaque.

Far right, catcher Johnny Roseboro, a respectable replacement for Campanella, appeared on this Sixties pin.

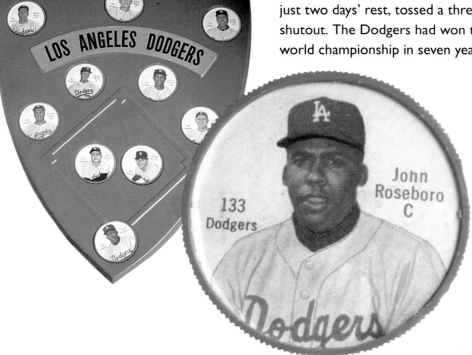

The Dynamic Duo, Koufax and Drysdale, quickened the pulse of all Dodger fans when they held out for a package salary deal in 1966, resulting in the first $100,000 salaries for pitchers. In their careers, Drysdale and Koufax together won 272 games, four Cy Young awards, 20 games in five seasons, and were named to 14 All-Star squads.

In the 1960s we had a great team. It was team effort every day, every night. We didn't have stars. We had a team that was a star.

—DON DRYSDALE, DODGERS

If the sports pages were full of one kind of drama during the 1965 Series, they were full of another kind during spring training in 1966, when Koufax and Drysdale staged the Great Holdout. The year before, Sandy Koufax had complained about his $70,000 salary, and in 1966 he was even unhappier over the offer from Dodger brass. He wanted very much to be a $100,000 pitcher, and, coming off a sensational year, he thought he should be. His teammate Drysdale, every bit as good as Koufax—and certainly as valuable at crunch time—had the same idea.

According to Drysdale, the two discussed their salary impasses and decided that they should negotiate together—one for all and all for one. It had never been done before, but no two pitchers on the same team had ever been as dynamic as these two, not since Dizzy and Daffy Dean

A ticket stub from a Dodgers tour of Japan in the Sixties.

in the Thirties. The pair reportedly demanded $500,000 each for three years, while management reportedly offered each $95,000 for one year. Today Roger Clemens gets over $4 million a year, but in 1966, no pitcher in the business earned $100,000, although that amount was paid to Mantle, Mays, Musial, and Williams. And in 1966 there was no free agency; that was still nine years away. Through the reserve clause, your team owned you forever and paid you what it pleased.

Back at the Dodgers' training camp, neither side budged. Koufax and Drysdale had two aces in the hole: neither of them would report to spring training without a contract, and they threatened to use a recent court ruling on movie contracts that outlawed a studio from holding an actor to a contract after seven years to force the issue of free agency in baseball. The Dodgers had two aces in the hole: public opinion, which was shifting slowly in management's favor, and the regulation that said Koufax and Drysdale could play baseball nowhere else.

Weeks passed and nothing happened. Finally, Bavasi tired of talking and the duo tired of holding out. At the last minute, just before the end of spring training, the pitchers caved in and signed one-year deals that reportedly gave Koufax $125,000 and Drysdale $115,000.

Sports Heroes magazine was not going to overlook Sandy Koufax in its 1966 edition. And *Life* put Sandy on one of its '63 covers after he wasted the Yankees in the World Series.

Although they lost their effort to establish lucrative three-year deals, they did crack the $100,000 barrier. Were they worth it? In his book, *Once a Bum, Always a Dodger,* Drysdale wrote that someone showed him statistics that revealed an 8,000-fan jump in attendance each time Koufax pitched and a 3,000-fan jump when he pitched. Multiplying that attendance times $4.50 a person in tickets, parking, and food, times 30 starts per pitcher adds up to $1 million in additional Dodgers revenue for each hurler on $120,000 in salary. Not bad.

With the holdout over, Koufax went right back to mowing down the National League, taking the Dodgers to yet another pennant in 1966 with 27 wins and an astonishing 1.73 ERA. He frequently complained of a sore arm, but no one thought much of it. Drysdale, on the other hand, had a bad year, finishing at 13-16. As usual, the Dodgers had to battle the fierce San Francisco Giants all season to win the pennant. No team played as well as the Giants that decade, averaging nearly 90 wins a year, but no team had so little to show for it. In the World Series, L.A., tired of the long season and a six-month battle with the Giants, fell to the Baltimore Orioles in four straight.

In the spring of 1967 the biggest

114

Far left, the Dodgers often featured their stadium in pennants like this 1966 World Series number.

Left, the Dodgers failed to repeat in 1966—Baltimore swept them in four.

Below, no. 32 (Koufax) won 165 and lost 87 in a career cut short by injury. The mercurial pitcher, still trim and tanned with some spots of gray in his hair, was elected to the Hall of Fame in 1972.

bombshell since O'Malley announced he was leaving Brooklyn exploded on Dodgers fans. Sandy Koufax, just 31, suddenly retired from baseball, no longer able to take the constant pain from the arthritis that had developed in his pitching arm. The best pitcher in baseball over the previous decade was gone.

Fleet-footed Maury Wills, traded after he took an unauthorized leave of absence during a postseason tour of Japan, was also gone. Hard hitting but injured Tommy Davis was traded to the Mets. Junior Gilliam stopped playing and moved to coaching (for the second time). Lou Johnson, a guardian angel for the team in 1965, broke an ankle. Mentally, emotionally, and physically, the Dodgers hobbled into the 1967 season and out the other end, finishing eighth that year and seventh in 1968.

The highlight of 1968, of course, was Drysdale's record 58 2/3 consecutive scoreless innings, not broken until Orel Hershiser came along 20 years later. But right after the end of his 14-12 season, injuries started to affect Drysdale, too, and he retired at the end of the 1969 season. The Dodgers were a mournful blue when their big ace, who had won 209 games and pitched in eight All-Star contests, left the rotation. An era ended.

Red Machine. But the fans didn't have long to wait—the Dodgers were never going to stay down long again.

Many things were changing as the 1970s began. After ten long years of experimentation, America had finally landed men on the moon in the summer of 1969. Richard Nixon assumed the presidency that year, even as students across the country protested the Vietnam war and seized university buildings. Many of the television shows that originated in New York, like Johnny Carson's *Tonight Show,* were relocating to Los Angeles.

Baseball changed in 1969 and 1970, too, and it wasn't just the taking of the pennant by the Miracle Mets with their madhouse fans. Four more teams entered the big leagues—the San Diego Padres and Montreal Expos in the National League and the Kansas City Royals and Seattle Pilots (now the Milwaukee Brewers) in the American. Each league was split into two divisions, and a playoff between two divisions rather than season records would determine the pennant winner. To complete the shake-up, the pitcher's mound was lowered and the strike zone was shrunk.

With Koufax and Drysdale gone along with some of the stronger hitters,

A collection of late Sixties and early Seventies scorecards.

The National League was split into Eastern and Western divisions in 1969, although that just meant that the Dodgers finished fourth instead of eighth. In 1970 they did crawl back to second, which still put them 14 games behind Cincinnati's Big

the Dodgers needed new power on the mound and new strength at the plate. So once again, as in the days of Larry MacPhail, the club looked down into its wonderfully well organized and efficient farm system. The Dodgers had been mining solid gold baseball ore out of there for years and several important players were ready for the jump to the bigs.

Bill Russell, just 20, was called up from Bakersfield. Steve Garvey, a muscular first baseman, was brought up from Albuquerque, and Bill Buckner arrived from Ogden, Utah. Ted Sizemore was brought up from Spokane and Wills, forgiven for wandering in Japan, was brought back. Veteran Manny Mota came over from the Padres (and he would set

records as a pinch hitter). Fans dubbed the primarily young lineup, most of whom sported sideburns, "the Mod Squad."

In the front office, Walter O'Malley promoted his son Peter to chief executive officer; the younger O'Malley would do as much for Los Angeles baseball as his father did. More trades were made in 1970 and at the start of the 1971 season the new general manager, Al Campanis, signed muscular slugger Richie Allen, who had hit over 30 home runs each of the last three years. Brawny Ron Cey and Davey Lopes came up from the minors; along with Garvey, one of the country's most gifted athletes, and Russell, they would soon make up baseball's best infield since the 1963 Yankees.

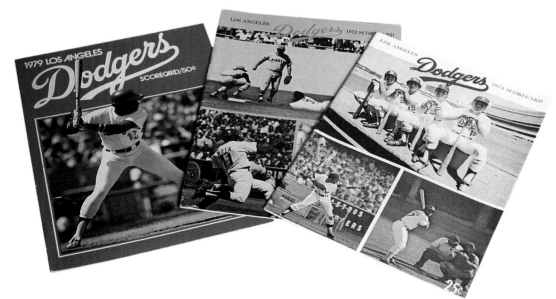

Dodgers programs added more pictures as the Seventies rolled by.

DODGER STADIUM

No matter where you sit in gorgeous Dodger Stadium, you marvel that it's in the center of one of America's largest cities. The best views are of the mountains from behind first base and downtown from behind third.

GUEST
GRAND OPENING
DODGER
STADIUM

HOME OF
THE
DODGERS
AND
ANGELS

APRIL
9
1962

A Dodger Stadium opening-day flag.

The Toronto Skydome may be baseball's most sophisticated ballpark, Fenway the most charming, and Yankee Stadium the most historic, but Dodger Stadium is certainly the most beautiful. It sits in the center of a 300-acre site that gives fans a sensational view of the green hills and palm trees beyond the outfield and a spectacular nighttime view of downtown Los Angeles. But it wasn't always that way. When O'Malley started purchasing Chavez Ravine piece by piece in 1958, it was a desolate area full of hills, ledges, gullies, and washes. Yet when Dodger Stadium opened there in 1962 it was an

It took a collector three years to get over a hundred past and present Dodgers to sign this home plate.

A Dodger Stadium souvenir salesman.

immediate success, drawing 2.75 million fans that first season. Now the 56,000-seat park is surrounded by gorgeous landscaping highlighted by over 2,000 Eucalyptus and Acacia trees, dozens of palms, and 300 Olympic rose bushes, all requiring ten full-time gardeners. With its manicured fields and immaculate seating areas, the stadium is baseball's botanical garden. Spacious, lush, and beautiful, Dodger Stadium represents a vivid contrast to marvelous old Ebbets Field and stands as a reminder to all the fans from the good old days that something new can be wonderful too.

The sleeves of his jersey barely contain the arms of muscular slugger Steve Garvey, who came out of nowhere to win the MVP award in 1974 (he had been such an unknown that year that he made the All-Star team as a write-in).

The budding new Dodgers, featuring pitchers Al Downing and Don Sutton, finished second, just a hair behind the Giants, who finally won a pennant title after nine years. Fans jammed Dodger Stadium that year, setting a major league attendance record of 3.6 million. The Dodgers struggled in third place in 1972, $10\frac{1}{2}$ games out, but finished a strong second the next season, just $3\frac{1}{2}$ games behind the Reds. The stage was set for their memorable 1974 year.

That season the Dodgers had their usual tremendous fan support, an aging but still-cagey Alston in the dugout, and a minor league system that was producing talent like the mint produces money. But

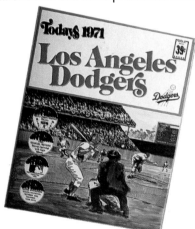

I have been a fan since I was ten seconds old. My father was an absolute nut about the Dodgers. I've loved the team all my life. Steve Garvey was the greatest athlete who ever lived.

—SEAN DEATON, FAN, LONG BEACH, CALIFORNIA

A program from 1971, the year the Dodgers came from 10 games back to almost catch the Giants on the last day of the season, losing the pennant by a single game.

they also had the best infield in the business. Back in 1912, when he managed the powerhouse Philadelphia A's, Connie Mack referred to his stellar infield as the $100,000 infield. Given inflation, this 1974 version was more of a million-dollar infield. The Dodgers also acquired ace reliever Mike Marshall. In short, Walt Alston, in the twilight years of his mild-mannered and remarkably productive

career, had a team to break the bank.

"In the early Seventies it was just a thrill to watch that infield. They were the best defensive infield in the game and they could produce at the plate. Baseball will never see another infield like it," said long-time fan Rose Ray, hurrying to her seat to catch the tail end of batting practice one recent night. Ray should know—she has seen every Dodgers infield since 1958 and

When the Dodgers moved to L.A. they became home team to the Hollywood movie and TV stars who flocked to the park to see them. Here Frank Sinatra, dressed in Dodger blue head to toe, visits Don Sutton in the locker room.

121

Mike Marshall, who earned three degrees at Michigan State, became the Dodger fire chief in 1974 when he appeared in a record 106 games, pitched a record 208 innings, and became the only pitcher in World Series history to finish off every game. His efforts won him the Cy Young Award, rarely given to relievers.

Photos from a "Picture Pack" fans could purchase in the Seventies.

minor league infields in Los Angeles back into the Forties.

The million-dollar infield was made up of Ron Cey at third, Bill Russell at short, Davey Lopes at second, and ball-cruncher Steve Garvey at first. They played together occasionally in 1973, but when the '74 season opened they formed the core of the team and remained so all through the Seventies and into the Eighties.

Reliever Mike Marshall provided the second half of the Dodgers' punch, complemented by a regular staff headed by Don Sutton, Andy Messersmith, and Tommy John. He had led the league in saves with 31 with Montreal the year before he arrived in Los Angeles. When the team's other top reliever, Jim Brewer, was injured, Marshall became the king of

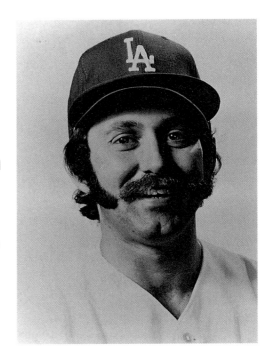

the hill, compiling an astonishing 15-12 record on a 2.42 ERA with 21 saves. During his career Iron Mike set major league records for appearances (106), most innings pitched in relief (208), most games finished (83), and consecutive games pitched (13). At the end of his first season with the Dodgers he became the first relief pitcher ever to win the Cy Young Award.

The Dodgers were hot right away. They won their first three games—8-0, 8-0, and 9-2—and kept streaking. The pitchers threw well and the batters hit even better. And better than anyone was

Steve Garvey wound up hitting .294 lifetime and made ten All-Star teams.

went on to become one of the most productive and consistent Dodgers of the Seventies. He played in 1,207 consecutive games, made the All-Star team ten times, and in 1978 became the first All-Star candidate ever to get more than four million votes. (He was also the All-Star MVP that year.) He won four Gold Gloves for his fielding and in a seven-year stretch got over 200 hits six times. Garvey could always be counted on in tight spots: he hit eight home runs and smacked 21 RBIs in playoff action, and was named MVP in the League Championship Series in 1978 and again in 1984.

The Dodgers were a powerhouse in 1974, winning 102 games. They held off a

25-year-old first baseman Steve Garvey. The strongman with the huge hands averaged .312, with 200 hits, 21 home runs, and 111 RBIs. Garvey hadn't always been such a dazzler. He had played only parts of the 1969, '70 and '71 seasons, followed in '72 by a lackluster .269 average over 96 games with just nine home runs. In 1973 his average went up to .304, and the next season he exploded.

Garvey was such a surprise in '74 that he made the All-Star team only as a write-in. By the end of the season everyone knew what had happened, and he was voted the National League's MVP. Garvey

The Dodgers printed an interesting press pass for the 1974 Series, but the team lost to the Oakland A's in five games.

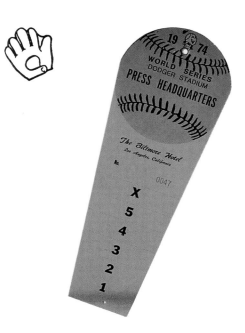

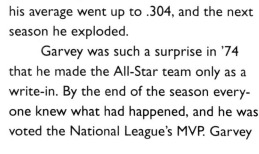

Three of L.A.'s championship flags.

late-season charge by the Reds and crushed the Pirates in the divisional play-offs. But they ran into a brick wall in the form of the Oakland A's in the Series. Led by Reggie Jackson, the A's were a tough bunch and beat the Dodgers, four games to one, in the first all-California world series.

There was much spring training talk of a rematch with the A's in the fall of 1975, but Cincinnati's Big Red Machine churned up the league that year, winning 108 games and finishing 20 games ahead of the second-place Dodgers. The Reds won the Series that year, beating Boston, and then finished ten games ahead of the Dodgers the next year before going on to win the Series again.

A scorecard from 1975, the year a pretty good Dodger team won a respectable 88 games and yet finished second by 20 games to Cincinnati's Big Red Machine, which won 108.

Back in 1932, when Wilbert Robinson retired after managing the Dodgers for 18 seasons, sportswriters declared that the

team would never again be managed that long by one man. But Walter Alston proved them wrong. Alston joined the Dodgers in Brooklyn in 1954, took them to their first World Series, and stayed at the helm for 23 long years. The quiet, casual manager was well liked in baseball and had become a community leader in Los Angeles. Finally, in the winter of 1977, he decided to retire. His successor was the volatile Tommy Lasorda who, like Alston, had been with the Dodger organization just about all of his adult life ("I did spend kindergarten in public school, however," he

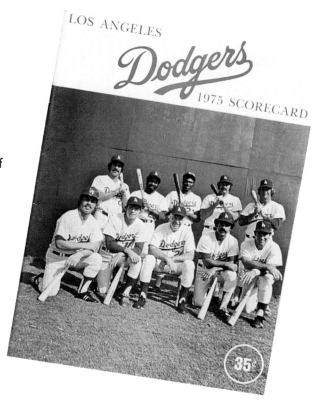

LOS ANGELES *Dodgers* 1975 SCORECARD

35¢

Tommy Lasorda celebrating his second World Series title, in 1988; he has also won four pennants. Asked which of his championship teams was the best, he said, "All of them."

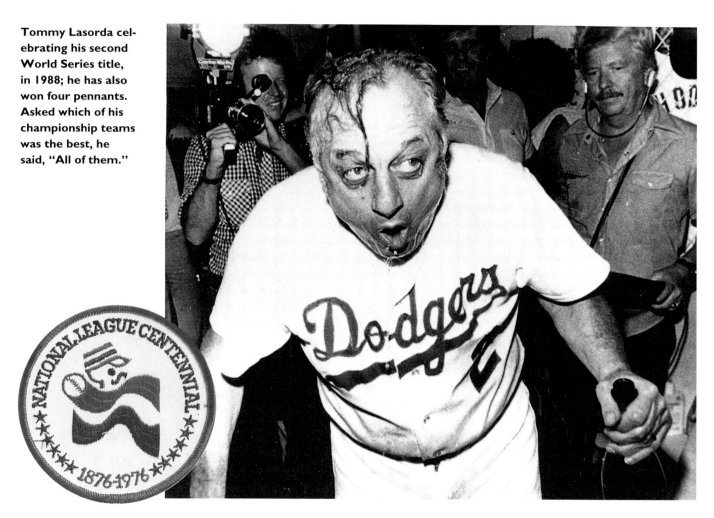

This centennial patch was sold in the Dodgers gift shop throughout 1976.

says). Lasorda had managed minor league teams as well as Puerto Rican, Cuban, Panamanian, and Dominican squads. Fluent in Spanish and English, the manager was a fiery dugout leader, the total opposite of quiet, composed Walt Alston. He cheered, yelled, and hugged his players. He argued umpires' calls with the ferocity of a wound-

ed lion. He was colorful and explosive, a whole new sideshow for fans.

And he was good. Under Lasorda the Dodgers raced out of the gate in 1977, winning 22 of their first 24 games. They kept racing, and at the end of the season they bested the fearsome Reds by ten games. Four Dodgers hit 30 or more home

125

runs (Steve Garvey, Reggie Smith, Ron Cey, and Dusty Baker). Cey had nine straight hits in a three-game series. Garvey, who had another super year with a .297 average and 115 RBIs, nailed five extra base hits in one game. Plus the pitching was superb: John was 20-7, Rick Rhoden 16-10, and Sutton 14-8.

In 1978, the Dodgers were just as good, winning another pennant (this time over the Reds by just 2 1/2 games). Garvey was becoming one of baseball's top first

The seventy-fifth anniversary of the World Series was not celebrated in L.A. after the Dodgers lost the Series to the Yanks in six.

CHAPTER SEVEN

FREEWAY FRENZY
1980 until Now

The Mexican Leagues have always constituted a parallel universe to American baseball. They have been around since the 1920s, when Negro League stars played there during the winter. In the 1940s they made headlines when several dozen major leaguers, lured by big money, left the States to play ball in Mexico a single season. In the 1950s major leaguers barnstormed there and some pitchers played there in the winter to stay sharp. The Mexican Leagues were always a footnote to something else.

In 1981, however, everyone found out about the Mexican Leagues and the talent playing there with the emergence of a 21-year-old kid named Fernando Valenzuela. The heavyset pitcher with the incredible screwball joined a team in the doldrums, a team that had finished a dismal fourth in 1980 and third in 1979. He joined them for one of the craziest seasons of all time and established himself as a superstar from the first day he danced his screwball through the air. Valenzuela won his first game of 1981 on a shutout and proceeded to win six straight, four on shutouts.

The reaction in Los Angeles was immediate. The likable Mexican superman, who spoke no English at first and communicated through an interpreter, ignited "Fernandomania," a wild love affair with the pitcher. By

Fernando Valenzuela had a lot to celebrate when he jumped from the Mexican League directly to the Dodgers and won Rookie of the Year honors in 1981. His arrival kicked off Fernandomania and brought thousands of Mexican-Americans to Dodger Stadium.

the Eighties the Mexican-American population of Los Angeles had grown tremendously, but the hundreds of thousands of Mexicans had no stake in the local baseball team. Not until one of their own not only joined it but became its star. Mexican-Americans began jamming Dodger Stadium to see the man who finally gave them a presence in their adopted city.

"That whole season was one big carnival for us," said fan Marno Tavarez, dressed in a sharp blue-and-white striped shirt. "Fernando was a folk hero."

Valenzuela would go on to pitch for ten years in Los Angeles, and he became the first pitcher awarded $1 million in arbitration. He won 60 percent of his games and once struck out five men in a row in an All-Star game. Most importantly, he served as a bridge for the dozens of Mexican and Latin American players who would pour into the majors in the Eighties and Nineties.

The 1981 season was a wild one. In the middle of it the players went on strike

A card set of 1980s Dodgers.

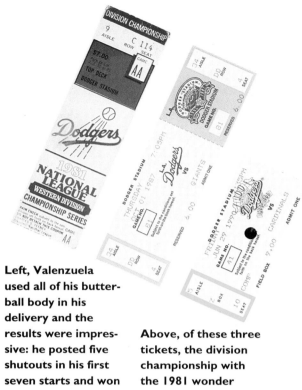

Left, Valenzuela used all of his butterball body in his delivery and the results were impressive: he posted five shutouts in his first seven starts and won the Cy Young Award as a rookie in 1981.

Above, of these three tickets, the division championship with the 1981 wonder team (*left*) is surely worth the most.

Valenzuela: He was the biggest hero the Mexican community here ever had. People planned their whole week around his pitching dates.

—MARIO TAVARAZ, DODGER STADIUM USHER

over free-agency regulations. So many games were lost that the leagues decided it was unfair to hold a traditional League Championship Series to determine the pennant, so they put together a half-baked scheme whereby the teams in first when the strike started would play the teams in first during the second part of the season to determine the division winners. This turned into a travesty when the Cincinnati Reds compiled the best record in baseball but were shut out of the championship series because they finished second in both halves of the season. The Dodgers were lucky. Even though they ended the

Top, a 1981 championship flag.

Right, pitcher Steve Howe jumps into catcher Steve Yeager's arms as Steve Garvey leaps in glee to celebrate the 1981 World Series win over the Yankees.

Below, the Dodgers won the 1981 Series, with knuckleballer Burt Hooton shutting down the Yankees in the sixth and final game.

Dodgers too, and Lasorda took his first world championship. The triumph was as sweet as they get, redemption for the many pennants and World Series the team should have won in the late Sixties and Seventies and revenge, sweetest of all, against their arch enemy, the Yankees.

"Probably my most satisfying Series win, given the long and crazy season and the long playoffs. And we beat a strong, strong Yankee team," said Lasorda.

The names on the jerseys started to change in the Eighties. The great infield of Russell, Cey, Lopes, and Garvey was split

The headline says it all as Dodgers win the 1981 Series following the strike-shortened season. The lords of baseball made the teams stage two playoffs to determine who got into the World Series that year, and when the Dodgers finally triumphed the champagne corks were popped with weary fingers.

Right, a 1982 twentieth-anniversary Dodger scorecard.

season in fourth place, they had been first before the strike and squeaked into the playoffs where they first beat Montreal, then Houston. The World Series was staged against the Yankees, and the Dodgers had their hands full. Not only did the Yankees have all their usual killers—Nettles, Jackson, Randolph—but on the mound they had none other than former Dodger Tommy John, purchased as a free agent. They were loaded.

As predicted the Yanks took the first two games, and it looked like a lock, but the spunky never-say-die Dodgers fought back gamely, winning game three 5-4 and game four 8-7. Then, on pitching, hitting, and just guts, the Dodgers grabbed game five. Finally, with Burt Hooton and then Howe on the mound, game six fell to the

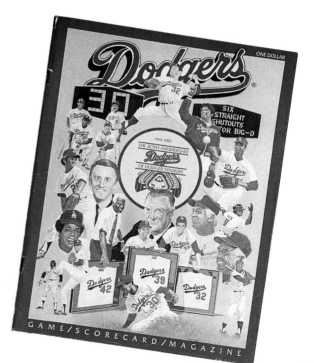

133

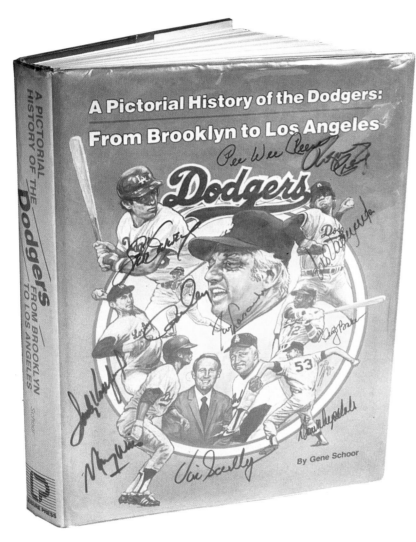

A Pictorial History of the Dodgers:
From Brooklyn to Los Angeles

Dodgers

By Gene Schoor

Manager Tommy Lasorda rightfully belongs in the center of this book cover. Since 1977 he has been the engine **of the Dodgers team. When asked how good a manager he is, he explained, "I make good pasta."**

up. The team finished second in 1982 but won the division the next year before losing the pennant to the Phillies. In '84 they slumped to fourth but roared back to win the division title in '85. They then slid to fifth in '86 and fourth in '87.

Through it all, the Dodgers were a stable and winning ball club, one of the most successful in the major leagues. "I remember the Eighties as a time when every day we fielded a TEAM. Lots of players came and went and the TEAM still won. Those ball clubs were all wonderful examples of teamwork," said Lasorda.

As always, the Dodgers still had pitching.

"If you study the history of the Dodgers in the late Seventies and 1980s, you see the keys are the arms of Valenzuela, Sutton, Tommy John, Orel Hershiser, Burt Hooton. Go back into the Sixties to Drysdale and Koufax," said catcher Gary Carter, who has played against them often. "Los Angeles has always been pitching rich. They have always had great talent on the mound and good relievers like Steve Howe and Mike Marshall. It's been the pitching that's made them a powerhouse."

Today's ballplayers pulled for each other, as Ramon Martinez, a pitcher nervous about moving up to the majors, discovered. His long fingers holding a ball

The Dodgers, to me, growing up in California, were the Cadillacs of baseball. Everything about them was first class. I even thought their royal blue colors were the best colors in baseball. When I was a kid I'd dream of being a Dodger one day. The first day I put this jersey on I thought I was in heaven.

—BRETT BUTLER, DODGERS

Above, a Dodger dog from the 1980s.

Upper right, Tommy Lasorda signed this ball for a fan in 1990.

I want my players to win, but I want them to be happy. I want them to want to play baseball. I want a guy to look at that clock on his kitchen wall and say to his wife, "Look at that—only 45 minutes until I can go to the ballpark and play baseball for the Dodgers." That's my job—to motivate that player, to bring out the best in him. If I can do that, I'm doing a good job.

—TOMMY LASORDA, Dodgers manager

135

If there is one thing that was special about the Dodgers in the Eighties, and today, the players have an unshakable belief that they will win the ball game. Doesn't matter if they are behind 9-1, they feel they can still win the ball game. You don't get that kind of spirit in all teams.

—DUKE SNIDER, DODGERS

and his curly black hair hanging down from the back of his cap, Martinez talked lovingly of his teammates, for whom he won 20 games in 1990.

"These guys want to win for themselves, but they want to win for you, too," said Martinez. "I could never have had the success I have enjoyed here without guys who were always trying to win for me, to get an extra hit for me, that one run that makes the difference."

But Lasorda was the glue of the Eighties teams, and he remains so today. Good ballplayers were eager to pull on a bright blue lettered jersey. "He's the kind of guy you want to win for," enthused slugger Darryl Strawberry. "You don't just

want to win for the fans, or the ball club, which is what it's like on most teams. You want to win for Tommy."

As the Dodgers continued to win division titles, pennants, and world championships in the Eighties, the Dodgers' legend grew. "Don't think it's schmaltzy, but my dream in life was to grow up and play for the Dodgers," admitted Brett Butler. "To me, to most people, they are the elite, the very best team, the very best organization. When things didn't work out for me with the Giants and I had the chance to play here, I jumped at it."

Indeed they did so well that everyone else started training their guns on them.

"I think what happened is this," said Lasorda as he sat on a plastic seat cushion in the Dodgers dugout. "We always had that rivalry with the Giants, and still do. Then, to stay on top, we had to always beat the Cards, and beat the Reds. So with all those games, key series, playoff matchups, the Dodgers were developing longtime rivalries with many teams. Let's face it, if you want to win the division or the pennant, you've got to get by us. Therefore, we are targets for everybody. Everybody wants to beat us. It's like the old Yankees."

The Dodgers always had heart, and that, more than anything else, propelled them past the powerful Mets in a seven-

Above, pitcher Orel Hershiser made history in 1988 when he finished the year with 59 scoreless innings to break Don Drysdale's 20-year record. The mild-mannered Hershiser then tossed eight more scoreless innings against the Mets in the league championship series. He won two games in the 1988 World Series and even went three for three in the one game in which he batted.

Right, the media jumped on Orel in 1988 like they had on Sandy 20 years before. The pitcher won 23 games that year.

137

DODGER FANS

What fans could live without their very own Matchbox Dodgers truck?

A patch from the early 1970s.

Most stadiums' souvenir sales are based directly on winning or losing. If the team wins, people are happy and buy things. If the team loses, they don't. Here it's not like that. People buy Dodger memorabilia whether they win or not. Sometimes they'll get killed, like 10-1 or something, and we'll have a huge night. People just like the team, that's all.

—MARK McCOOL,
DODGER STADIUM SOUVENIR SALESMAN

When I was a teenager, I made up my mind I would be the first woman who ever played for the Dodgers. I wanted to play for the best team in baseball and they were it . . . and still are.

—SANDRA ZERNE, FAN AND STAR SECOND BASEMAN FOR THE RISING FORCE SOFTBALL TEAM, LOS ANGELES

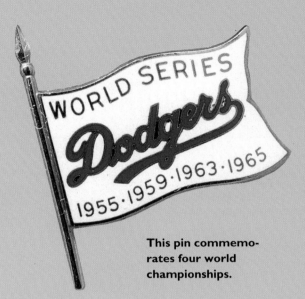

This pin commemorates four world championships.

I know nothing about baseball, but my friends said I should be a Dodger fan.

—JELENA KAROVIC OF YUGOSLAVIA AT HER VERY FIRST BASEBALL GAME

I've been a Dodger fan since 1955, when we used to go see the Dodger farm club in Bakersfield play. Don Drysdale pitched for them that summer. He knocked down everybody back then, too. I'll be a Dodger fan till I die. Who else would I root for?

—GEORGE ROSE, FAN, LOS ANGELES

Over eighty Dodgers signed this bat at the request of an ambitious collector.

A program and tickets for the dramatic 1988 World Series, in which an ailing Kirk Gibson made history by winning game one with a last-inning home run.

MAJOR LEAGUE BASEBALL

OFFICIAL PROGRAM $5.00

1988 World Series

OAKLAND Athletics vs. NATIONAL LEAGUE CHAMPIONS

GAME FOUR

SEC ROW SEAT
118-35-10
FIELD BOX
GAME FOUR
50.00

1988 World Series

DODGER STADIUM
GAME
1 $50.00
FIELD BOX
1988 WORLD SERIES

1988 World Series Dodgers vs. AMERICAN LEAGUE CHAMPIONS

GAME
1

My father had five sons. A man once asked him which one he liked the most. He refused to answer. He said he might as well cut off one of his five fingers. You can't ever say one [Dodgers] team was better than another. That's like comparing Ruth and DiMaggio or Mays and Canseco. Can't do it. I've had World Series champs, pennant winners. Which one was the best? They all were.

—TOMMY LASORDA, DODGERS MANAGER

game pennant series in 1988 and into the World Series against an Oakland A's team staffed with sluggers Mark McGwire and José Canseco, and pitching stars Dennis Eckersley and Dave Stewart. The Dodgers garnered tremendous fan support as they transformed themselves from the sluggish fourth place team of the previous summer into a streaking ball club in 1988.

No one was hotter than reed-thin pitcher Orel Hershiser, an extraordinarily gifted hurler who looked like anything but a ballplayer. To put some grit into mild-mannered Hershiser, Lasorda had jokingly nicknamed him "Bulldog" when he came up in 1985. On the mound, he was. From '85 through '88 he averaged 18 wins a season, but it was 1988 that was Orel Hershiser's year, the kind of year Christy Mathewson had in 1908, Dizzy Dean in 1934, and Bob Gibson in 1967. Hershiser won 23 games that year and as the long season drew to a slow close he got better and better. He ended the season brilliantly, going 10 scoreless innings in the season's final game for 59 straight scoreless innings—a record that easily broke Don Drysdale's mark of 58. He then went eight more scoreless innings in the playoffs.

Hershiser would be the mainstay of the World Series, just as he was in the playoffs (he was named MVP in both), but the 1988 Series would be remembered

Below, the 1988 pennants were some of the glitziest ever.

In one of sports' most memorable moments, a limping Kirk Gibson crushes a ninth-inning home run over the right field wall to win the first game of the 1988 World Series.

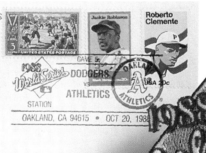

Above and right, manufacturers worked overtime to produce patches and first-day covers following the 1988 world championship.

Right, Darryl Strawberry grew up in Los Angeles and came back to play for the Dodgers in 1991 after a successful but unhappy career in New York with the Mets. Although popular with the fans, Strawberry hasn't done much because of chronic injuries.

Below, a first-day cover signed by Orel Hershiser.

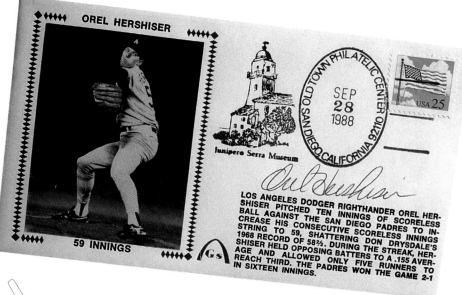

OREL HERSHISER

59 INNINGS

SEP 28 1988
OLDTOWN PHILATELIC CENTER 0126
SAN DIEGO, CALIFORNIA
Junipero Serra Museum
USA 25

LOS ANGELES DODGER RIGHTHANDER OREL HERSHISER PITCHED TEN INNINGS OF SCORELESS BALL AGAINST THE SAN DIEGO PADRES TO INCREASE HIS CONSECUTIVE SCORELESS INNINGS STRING TO 59, SHATTERING DON DRYSDALE'S 1968 RECORD OF 58⅔. DURING THE STREAK, HERSHISER HELD OPPOSING BATTERS TO A .155 AVERAGE AND ALLOWED ONLY FIVE RUNNERS TO REACH THIRD. THE PADRES WON THE GAME 2-1 IN SIXTEEN INNINGS.

forever for one swing of Dodger outfielder Kirk Gibson's bat. Going into post season play the Dodgers were underdogs, but they stunned the sports world by winning the pennant against the Mets, to whom they had lost 10 of 11 regular-season games. Gibson had played very well that year after being traded to L.A. by the Tigers, but he was sidelined with a serious leg injury. He limped all over the stadium offices before the game, testing his damaged leg; he could not play.

Grimacing in pain as he walked about the trainer's room, Gibson watched the first game on television. In the waning moments of the last inning the A's were ahead, 4-3, with one man on base and a red-hot Eckersley on the mound. Suddenly Gibson, not even dressed, yelled to a bat boy to tell Lasorda he wanted to pinch hit. Lasorda, sensing something, sent him up.

The roar from the crowd in Dodger Stadium on a fine October night drowned out the sounds of freeway traffic as Gibson limped badly into the batter's box. He worked the count to 3-2, wincing on a foul ball, and then, in an ending better than the movies, crashed a towering home run over the right-field fence to win the game. He had to hobble around the bases, pumping his arms in joy; by the time he neared the plate he could barely walk, but fans could have cheered him all night.

The rest of the Series was a little anti-climactic. Hershiser pitched brilliantly, the team hit well, and Lasorda made his usual shrewd decisions, but Gibson had provided the kind of drama fans thrive on, the kind of drama baseball was made for. The Dodgers took the Series and were crowned world champions once again.

Gibson was the Dodgers' hero that night in 1988, but the team has had heroes for over 100 years. Valenzuela—a legend after one season. Hershiser—a legend with 67 innings of scoreless ball. And ranging back over the

Dodger blue doesn't get any deeper than this recent felt patch.

years, Hodges, Koufax, Drysdale, Campanella, Robinson, Reese, Snider. . . .

New heroes are accepted as easily as old ones are venerated. No one knows that better than Darryl Strawberry, the unhappy Met who was traded to the Dodgers in 1991. "The people here like players who work hard and try their best. That's all they want," he said. "We try to play our best all the time for them. That's why the Dodgers are such a great team.

"Look out there at those guys," Straw continued, waving a bat he was swinging in pregame batting practice toward the field. "Martinez, Hershiser, Butler, Juan Samuel. . . . These are some of the best players in the country and they're here on one team. The Dodgers have tradition every year."

In the mists of Chavez Ravine, you could almost see the ghost of Charlie Ebbets nodding his approval of Strawberry's assessment and looking around in the hills to see where they put the trolley out here.

DODGER GREATS

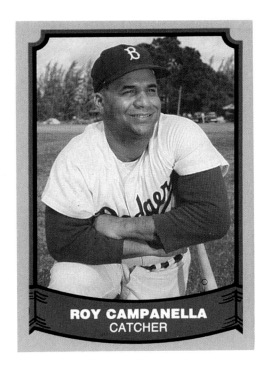

ROY CAMPANELLA
CATCHER

WALTER ALSTON

The backbone of the Dodgers over the years, in Brooklyn and Los Angeles, has been the team's managers. Unlike most teams, the Dodgers have stuck with their managers and their faith has paid off. One of the very best was Walt Alston, a quiet, unassuming skipper with a great eye for talent and a keen understanding of the game. He adapted to his teams rather than forcing them to adapt to him, winning world championships with good hitting clubs (1950s), good mound staffs (1960s), and untested young players (1970s). Alston, who played minor league ball for 13 years, joined the Dodgers in 1954 and took them to seven World Series. He was voted Manager of the Year six times and won with seven of the eight All-Star teams he was named to manage. Alston served as skipper of the Dodgers longer than anyone—23 years—and was elected to the Hall of Fame in 1983.

ROY CAMPANELLA

Campy started playing professional baseball as a 15-year-old schoolboy with the Negro Leagues' Bacharach Giants and then moved to the Baltimore Elite Giants. By 1946, when he was signed by the Dodgers and sent to a farm club in New Hampshire, he was hitting over .300 regularly and was recognized by most as the best catcher in the country. Indeed he was so experienced that when the farm team manager (Walt Alston) was sick or had been ejected from a game he always appointed Campanella interim manager.

Like many Negro League stars, who had little coaching and played every-day schedules, Campanella improved in the majors.

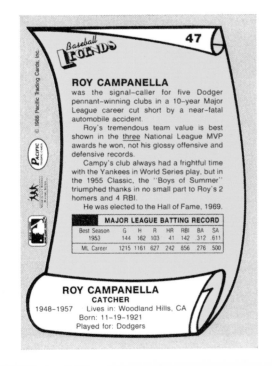

47

ROY CAMPANELLA
was the signal-caller for five Dodger pennant-winning clubs in a 10-year Major League career cut short by a near-fatal automobile accident.

Roy's tremendous team value is best shown in the three National League MVP awards he won, not his glossy offensive and defensive records.

Campy's club always had a frightful time with the Yankees in World Series play, but in the 1955 Classic, the "Boys of Summer" triumphed thanks in no small part to Roy's 2 homers and 4 RBI.

He was elected to the Hall of Fame, 1969.

MAJOR LEAGUE BATTING RECORD								
Best Season	G	H	R	HR	RBI	BA	SA
1953	144	162	103	41	142	.312	.611
ML Career	1215	1161	627	242	856	.276	.500

ROY CAMPANELLA
CATCHER
1948–1957   Lives in: Woodland Hills, CA
Born: 11-19-1921
Played for: Dodgers

He won the MVP title in three of his ten seasons and became a consistent World Series star for the Dodgers. Although he only hit .276 lifetime for the Dodgers, he smacked 242 home runs with 856 RBIs. His easy-going, winning personality off the field made him a beloved Dodger and helped gain acceptance for more blacks in the majors.

In 1958 Campanella was paralyzed for life in an automobile accident that cut a good five years off his career. But his highly publicized positive attitude following the tragedy made him even more of a fan favorite across America. Today, in his early seventies, he is a familiar figure at spring training and at Dodger Stadium games.

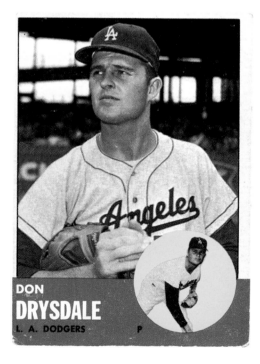

DON
DRYSDALE
L. A. DODGERS   P

TOPPS 360 DON DRYSDALE Pitcher · L. A. Dodgers

HT: 6:06 WT: 205 THROWS: Right
BATS: Right BORN: July 23, 1936
HOME: Van Nuys, Cal.

Don blossomed into a top star last year as he finally lived up to his potential. The ace pitched 19 complete games and led the majors in strikeouts.

FINE HITTER, DON HIT 7 HOMERS IN 1958

COMPLETE MAJOR AND MINOR LEAGUE PITCHING RECORD

YEAR	TEAM	LEA.	G	IP	W	L	PCT	SO	BB	ERA
1954	Bakersfield	Calif.	15	112	8	5	.615	73	58	3.45
1955	Montreal	Int.	28	173	11	11	.500	80	68	3.33
1956	Brooklyn	N. L.	25	99	5	5	.500	55	31	2.64
1957	Brooklyn	N. L.	34	221	17	9	.654	148	61	2.69
1958	Los Angeles	N. L.	44	212	12	13	.480	131	72	4.16
1959	Los Angeles	N. L.	44	271	17	13	.567	242	93	3.45
1960	Los Angeles	N. L.	41	269	15	14	.517	246	72	2.84
1961	Los Angeles	N. L.	40	244	13	10	.565	182	83	3.69
1962	Los Angeles	N. L.	43	314	25	9	.735	232	78	2.84
Major League Totals	7 Yrs.		271	1630	104	73	.588	1236	490	3.21

©T.C.G. PRINTED IN U.S.A.

DON DRYSDALE

Big D teamed up with Sandy Koufax in the early 1960s to give the Dodgers one of the best 1-2 mound combinations in baseball history. The team finished first five out of six years at their peak, from 1962 to 1967. Drysdale combined a good fastball, delivered sidearm, with consistent location to baffle batters for 12 years. He won 209 games and earned a well deserved reputation as a workhorse, leading the league in starts four years in a row.

Drysdale won the Cy Young Award in 1962 and was named to eight All Star teams, but the unquestioned highlight of his career came in 1968 when he hurled 58 scoreless innings to set a record. He was one of the better hitters in baseball pitching history, leading all National League hurlers in home runs four times. He was elected to the Hall of Fame in 1984.

LEO DUROCHER

Leo the Lip Durocher—the only man in baseball with four proper names—was affectionately known by Dodgers and Giants fans as "the Lip" because he spent most of his adult life arguing with umpires. A flashy dresser who married glamorous Hollywood actress Larraine Day, Durocher also managed the Cubs from 1966 to 1972 and the Astros in 1972 and 1973. Although he was an exceptionally effective coach, he is best remembered as the author of the famous line "Nice guys finish last" (about his friend Mel Ott, whose Giants were in the cellar), and for quashing a Dodgers' players petition to forbid Jackie Robinson to enter baseball in 1947; at a midnight meeting Durocher told the five culprits that "every man who signs will be traded before breakfast." Although he has never been inducted into the Hall of Fame, Durocher is considered by players and fellow managers to have been one of the best skippers in the game.

GIL HODGES

Few remember that the great first baseman originally came up as a catcher. The arrival of Campanella gave him the chance to try first, however, and there he proved to be a natural. The muscular slugger with huge hands hit 20 or more home runs eleven times and 100 or more RBIs seven straight seasons. With his easy smile and gentle disposition, Hodges became an eight-time All-Star.

He also went on to be a fine manager. After an unsuccessful stint with the Washington Senators, he came to the hapless New York Mets and managed them to a miracle world championship in 1969. A third- and a fourth-place finish followed, and then, in spring training of 1972, the 47-year-old Hodges died of a heart attack. All of baseball mourned and prayers were said for weeks in churches throughout Brooklyn.

SANDY KOUFAX

The *K* in *Koufax* may have stood for strikeout, but Sandy K. got off to a mediocre start as a pitcher with the Dodgers, going through several lackluster seasons until 1961, when he exploded with an 18-13 record and a National League-leading 269 strikeouts. The next year he was 14-7, and in 1962 he established himself as the best pitcher in baseball with a 27-5 mark.

Blessed with a blinding fastball, Sandy hurled no-hitters every season from 1962 to 1965; struck out a record 382 batters in '65, and won 165 games, most in his last six years, before a sudden arm injury ended his career. He won three Cy Young Awards, two of them back to back, and pitched in six All Star games. He was elected to the Hall of Fame in 1972.

JACKIE ROBINSON

When Jackie Robinson became the first black player in the majors in 1947, he came under enormous pressure. Not only did he have to break the color line singlehandedly, but he had to play well. But the 28-year-old Rookie of the Year was sensational, hitting .297 with 12 home runs and a league leading 29 stolen bases (he stole home 19 times in his career and even did it once in the World Series). The most aggressive and electrifying player since Ty Cobb, Robinson opened the door to other blacks and altered the face of baseball. During a ten year career Jackie went on to average .311. He was elected to six consecutive All Star teams, was named Most Valuable Player in 1949 (when his .342 average led the league), and is considered one of the great second basemen of all time. He was elected to the Hall of Fame in 1962.

JACKIE ROBINSON

DUKE SNIDER

One of the most popular men in all baseball, Duke Snider hit 407 home runs, 1,333 RBIs, and ended his career with a .295 average. The Dodgers' leading slugger, he was immortalized in the song "Willie, Mickey, and the Duke," about New York's three Hall-of-Fame center fielders. He came up in 1947, but didn't catch fire until 1949, when a grooved swing helped him hit 23 homers. Snider became a key cog in the Dodgers machine that dominated the National League from 1947 through 1957 in Brooklyn, where the club won six pennants; he also provided strong support to Jackie Robinson as Robinson broke the color line in 1947. Since retirement, the Duke has spent most of his time as a broadcaster.

FERNANDO VALENZUELA

The pudgy pitcher was signed by the Dodgers in 1980 after several spectacular seasons in the Mexican leagues. He was an instant success on the mound, winning ten straight in his rookie year, and at the box office as well. His success started "Fernandomania," an epidemic that swept the large Mexican-American community in Los Angeles and sent Dodgers ticket sales soaring.

Fernando won both Rookie of the Year and Cy Young Award honors in 1981 and in 1983 he became the first player awarded $1 million a year in arbitration. He went on to win over 150 games before his arm gave out in 1991.

DODGER STATS

DODGERS INDIVIDUAL RECORDS (SINCE 1890)

BATTING

Highest Batting Average	Babe Herman (.393)	1930
Highest Slugging Percentage	Babe Herman (.678)	1930
Highest On-Base Percentage	Babe Herman (.455)	1930
Most Games	Maury Wills (165)	1962
Most Games (Brooklyn)	Carl Furillo, Gil Hodges (158)	1951
Most At-Bats	Maury Wills (695)	1962
Most At-Bats (Brooklyn)	Carl Furillo (667)	1951
Most Runs	Hub Collins (148)	1890
	Babe Herman (143)	1930*
Most Hits	Babe Herman (241)	1930
Most Singles	Wee Willie Keeler (187)	1899
	Wee Willie Keeler (179)	1900*
	Maury Wills (179)	1962
Most Doubles	John Frederick (52)	1929
Most Triples	George Treadway (26)	1894
	Hy Myers (22)	1920*
Most Home Runs (Left-Hander)	Duke Snider (43)	1956
Most Home Runs (Right-Hander)	Gil Hodges (42)	1954
Most Home Runs at Home	Gil Hodges (25)	1954
	Duke Snider (25)	1956
Most Home Runs on the Road	Gil Hodges (21)	1951
Most Grand Slams	Kal Daniels (3)	1990*
Most Extra Base Hits	Babe Herman (94)	1930
Most Total Bases	Babe Herman (416)	1930
Most Runs Batted In	Tommy Davis (153)	1962
Most Runs Batted In (Brooklyn)	Roy Camanella (142)	1953
Most Walks	Eddie Stanky (148)	1945
Most Strikeouts	Bill Grabarkewitz (149)	1970
Most Strikeouts (Brooklyn)	Dolph Camilli (115)	1941
Fewest Strikeouts (150 Games)	Jim Johnson (15)	1923
Most Times Hit by Pitch	Lou Johnson (16)	1965
Most Times Hit by Pitch (Brooklyn)	Jackie Robinson (14)	1952
Most Sacrifices (incl. sacrifice flies)	Jake Daubert (39)	1915
Most Sacrifice Hits	Jim Casey (32)	1907
Most Sacrifices Flies	Gil Hodges (19)	1954
Most Stolen Bases	Maury Wills (104)	1962
Most Stolen Bases (Brooklyn)	Monte Ward (88)	1892
	Jimmy Sheckard (67)	1903*
Most Pinch-Hits	Sid Gautreaux (16)	1936
Most Grounded into Double Plays	Carl Furillo (27)	1956
Fewest Grounded into Double Plays	Pete Reiser (0)	1942

PITCHING

Most Victories (Right-Hander)	Tom Lovett (30)	1890
	Joe McGinnity (29)	1900*
Most Victories (Left-Hander)	Sandy Koufax (27)	1966
Highest Winning Percentage (L.A.)	Phil Regan (.933)	1966
Highest Winning Percentage (Brooklyn)		
	Fred Fitzsimmons (.889)	1940
Highest Winning Percentage (20-game winner)		
	Preacher Roe (.880)	1951
Lowest Earned Run Average	Rube Marquard (1.58)	1916
Most Games Lost	George Bell (27)	1910
Most Games	Mike Marshall (106)	1974
Most Games (Brooklyn)	Clem Labine (62)	1956
Most Games Started	Bill Terry (44)	1890
	George Haddock (44)	1892
	Brickyard Kennedy (44)	1893*
	Don Drysdale (42)	1963, 1965
Most Complete Games	Brickyard Kennedy (40)	1893*
	Oscar Jones (38)	1904
Most Games Finished	Mike Marshall (83)	1974
Most Games Finished (Brooklyn)	Clem Labine (47)	1956
Most Innings Pitched	Brickyard Kennedy (382.2)	1893*
	Oscar Jones (377.0)	1904
Most Saves	Jay Howell (28)	1989
Most Strikeouts	Sandy Koufax (382)	1965
Most Strikeouts (Brooklyn)	Dazzy Vance (262)	1924
Most Base on Balls	Bill Donovan (151)	1901
Most Hits Batsman	Joe McGinnity (41)	1900
Most Wild Pitches	Sandy Koufax (17)	1958
Most Wild Pitches (Brooklyn)	Larry Cheney (15)	1916
Most Runs	Harry McIntyre (188)	1905
Most Earned Runs	Burleigh Grimes (138)	1925
Most Hits	Joe McGinnity (364)	1900
Most Home Runs	Don Sutton (38)	1970
Most Home Runs (Brooklyn)	Don Newcombe (35)	1955
Most Shut Outs (Left-Hander)	Sandy Koufax (11)	1963
Most Shut Outs (Right-Hander)	Don Sutton (9)	1972
Most Shut Outs (Brooklyn)	Burleigh Grimes (7)	1918
	Whitlow Wyatt (7)	1941

*SINCE 1900

149

DODGER STATS

DODGERS ALL-TIME PITCHING LEADERS

WINS

Sutton	233
Drysdale	209
Vance	190
Kennedy	174
Koufax	165
Grimes	158
Osteen	147
Valenzuela	141
Podres	136
Rucker	134

LOSSES

Sutton	181
Drysdale	166
Kennedy	150
Rucker	134
Vance	131
Osteen	126
Grimes	121
Valenzuela	116
Podres	104
Mungo	99

GAMES

Sutton	550
Drysdale	518
Brewer	474
Perranoski	457
Labine	425
Hough	401
Koufax	397
Kennedy	381
Vance	378
Podres	366

ERA
(1,100+ Innings)

Pfeffer	2.31
Rucker	2.43
Hershiser	2.71
Koufax	2.76
Smith	2.91
Drysdale	2.95
Scanlan	2.96
John	2.98
Singer	3.03
Osteen	3.09

SAVES

Brewer	125
Perranoski	101
Labine	83
Howell	65
Niedenfuer	64
Hough	60
Howe	59
Casey	50
Roebuck	43
Marshall	42

INNINGS

Sutton	3814
Drysdale	3432
Kennedy	2857
Vance	2758
Grimes	2426
Osteen	2397
Rucker	2375
Valenzuela	2348.2
Koufax	2324
Podres	2030

STRIKEOUTS

Sutton	2696
Drysdale	2486
Koufax	2396
Vance	1918
Valenzuela	1759
Podres	1331
Welch	1292
Rucker	1217
Osteen	1162
Hooton	1042

SHUTOUTS

Sutton	52
Drysdale	49
Koufax	40
Rucker	38
Osteen	34
Vance	30
Valenzuela	29
Pfeffer	25
Podres	23
Welch	23
Hershiser	23

COMPLETE GAMES

Kennedy	279
Vance	212
Grimes	205
Rucker	186
Drysdale	167
Pfeffer	157
Sutton	156
Koufax	137
Stein	136
McIntyre	119

DODGERS ALL-TIME BATTING LEADERS

GAMES

Wheat	2322
Russell	2181
Reese	2166
Hodges	2006
Gilliam	1956
Davis	1952
Snider	1923
Furillo	1806
Garvey	1727
Wills	1593

BATTING AVG (1800+ AB)

Keeler	360
Herman	339
Fournier	337
Wheat	317
Phelps	315
Mota	315
Jones	313
Robinson	311
Walker	311
Guerrero	309

AT-BATS

Wheat	8859
Reese	8058
Davis	7495
Russell	7318
Gilliam	7119
Hodges	6881
Snider	6640
Garvey	6543
Furillo	6378
Wills	6156

RUNS

Reese	1338
Wheat	1255
Snider	1199
Gilliam	1163
Hodges	1088
Davis	1004
Robinson	947
Furillo	895
Griffin	882
Wills	876

HITS

Wheat	2804
Reese	2170
Davis	2091
Snider	1995
Garvey	1968
Russell	1926
Furillo	1910
Gilliam	1889
Hodges	1884
Wills	1732

DOUBLES

Wheat	464
Snider	343
Garvey	333
Reese	330
Furillo	324
Davis	321
Gilliam	304
Hodges	294
Russell	293
Walker	274

TRIPLES

Wheat	171
Davis	110
Myers	97
Daubert	87
Snider	82
Hummel	82
Reese	80
Sheckard	76
Daly	76
Johnston	73

HOME RUNS

Snider	389
Hodges	361
Campanella	242
Cey	228
Garvey	211
Furillo	192
Guerrero	171
Davis	154
Baker	144
Camilli	139

RUNS BATTED IN

Snider	1271
Hodges	1254
Wheat	1223
Furillo	1058
Garvey	992
Reese	885
Campanella	856
Davis	849
Cey	842
Robinson	734

STOLEN BASES

Wills	490
Lopes	418
Davis	335
Sax	290
Griffin	264
Reese	232
Sheckard	212
Gilliam	203
Wheat	203
Robinson	197

BIBLIOGRAPHY

Allen, Maury. *Jackie Robinson: A Life Remembered.* New York: Franklin-Watts, 1987.

Alston, Walter. *Alston and the Dodgers.* New York: Doubleday, 1966.

Durocher, Leo. *The Dodgers and Me.* New York: Ziff Davis, 1948.

Fisher, David, and Tommy LaSorda. *The Artful Dodger.* New York: Avon, 1986.

Frommer, Harvey. *Rickey and Robinson: The Men Who Broke Baseball's Color Barrier.* New York: Macmillan, 1982.

Golenbock, Peter. *Bums: An Oral History of the Brooklyn Dodgers.* New York: Putnam, 1984.

Hershiser, Orel, and Jerry Jenkins. *Out of the Blue.* New York: Berkeley, 1989.

Kahn, Roger. *The Boys of Summer.* New York: Harper and Row, 1987.

Snider, Duke, and Bill Gilbert. *The Duke of Flatbush.* New York: Zebra, 1989.

Sullivan, Neil. *The Dodgers Move West.* New York: Oxford University Press, 1987.

Tygiel, Jules. *Baseball's Great Experiment: Jackie Robinson and His Legacy.* New York: Oxford University Press, 1983.

AUTOGRAPH PAGE

153

INDEX

PHOTOGRAPHY CREDITS

All photography is by David M. Spindel with the following exceptions:

Courtesy Alex's MVP Cards, New York: pp. 145 bottom, 147 top, 148 bottom; AP/Wide World Photos: pp. 59 top, 62, 70, 87 top, 90 top, 100, 104 top, 112, 137 left, 142 top; Bob Bartosz: p. 123 top left; Los Angeles Dodgers, Inc.: p. 121 (photo: Mark Malone); National Baseball Library, Cooperstown, N.Y.: pp. 10 top, 14, 24 top, 26 top, 27 left, 27 bottom right, 30 top, 31 bottom, 32 top right, 32 bottom, 34 top, 36, 37 bottom, 38 top, 45 left, 47 top, 50 top left, 53 top, 54 top, 73 left, 75 left, 76 right, 80, 85 top, 88, 94, 95 top, 98 left, 105 right, 107 top left, 108, 120 top left, 122 top right, 128, 131 left, 132 right; Reuters/Bettmann: p. 141 top right; Ernest Sisto: p. 79 left; UPI/Bettmann: pp. 29, 32 top left, 48, 57 right, 58 bottom, 60, 82 bottom left, 86 top, 125 right.